My Favorite Things

to see and share

V. GILBERT BEERS
RONALD A. BEERS

VICTOR

BOOKS a division of SP Publications, Inc.
WHEATON, ILLINOIS 60187

Offices also in
Whitby, Ontario, Canada
Amersham-on-the-Hill, Bucks, England

ARTISTS
Ann Iosa
Robert Korta
Luciana Peters
Blanche Sims
Suzanne Snider

Second printing, 1984

Library of Congress Catalog Card Number: 84-50134
ISBN: 0-88207-821-6

Manufactured in the United States of America

To Parents and Teachers

Not long ago we started a little game with friends and family. "What is your favorite memory?" we asked. We were surprised to hear the answers. Almost without exception we found (1) something from childhood, (2) something associated with the family doing happy things together, (3) something small, (4) something sensory rich, and (5) something that cost almost nothing.

If we know these things, why then do we not build more on them? Is it because we are too busy, too hurried, and for some reason do not put first things first?

Several recent secular books have focused on the erosion of childhood. These authors are concerned that we are forcing our children to grow up too fast. We are not letting children be children when they should.

As Christians we should be even more concerned about these things. In addition, we should be concerned that we are not giving children as much Bible teaching and Christian values when they should get them. We should be concerned that we must give our children the childhood delights many of us had, in the context of Christian living.

This book, like MY PICTURE BIBLE and CHOOSING GOD'S WAY, is written to help you restore those delights to your children, with a strong Christian message. MY FAVORITE THINGS focuses on those little things we rush by in our hurried life, which form an important part of the fabric of childhood.

These sensory rich little things build creativity and imagination. Couple that with the presence of a friend or family member and you have a strong life builder. Add yet another dimension, that these things should point the child to God, and you have the foundation for a strong Christian teaching program.

So these are our favorite things—the smell of pancakes to wake us, the muffled sound of a rooster in the morning, the soft touch of a baby chick, the beauty of Mother's smile, and the warmth of the fireplace as Grandfather tells his tale. Multiply these sights, sounds, and other sensory rich experiences, and you have those things which remind us of God who made them all. They remind us of family togetherness and the wonderful experience of read-to-me.

Come with us now and see if our favorite things will not become your favorite things too. Then give your child the beautiful gift of childhood—with God as its focus.

My Favorite Things
to see and share

Contents

5

It's That Time Again
My Favorite Thing: An Envelope

What do you think this girl and boy are doing? Are they sending Christmas cards? Is it Easter time? Why not? What do you see that tells you it is some other special time of the year? The boy is writing a note on his valentine. He is telling Grandmother and Grandfather that he loves them. Now he is ready to mail it. But wait! He needs something else. He can't just put the valentine in the mailbox. Do you see what he needs? The girl has already put her valentine in one. What is it?

A TIME TO SHARE

1. *What are the boy and girl doing?*
2. *Whose picture do you see?*
3. *What will the valentines tell them?*
4. *Do you think Mother will get one too?*

WHAT DO YOU SEE?
This boy and girl need: valentines, envelopes, pencils or pens to write, and a stamp to mail their valentines. Point to each one. What month is this?

Let's Fly a Kite
My Favorite Thing: My Kite

Can you feel the wind blowing? How does it feel when it blows on your face? It is making the tree branches go back and forth. It is making the grass bend over. This is a good day to fly a kite. That's why Father is here with his boy and girl. He is glad that he can do this with them. And the boy and girl are glad Father wants to be with them. It's fun to fly a kite on a windy day. So Father and the boy and girl are glad for a windy day. They are glad God made the wind. Are you?

WHAT DO YOU SEE?
Point to some things that blow in the wind. What keeps the kites from blowing away? Can you point to the string on each kite?

A TIME TO SHARE
1. *What kind of day is this?*
2. *Why are they glad for the wind?*
3. *Who sends the wind? Would you like to thank God for it?*

Splashing Time
My Favorite Thing: A Puddle

You can see that the rain is over. Now it is time to splash in this puddle. The boy and girl are having so much fun with their puppy. But look out! Here comes trouble. That other boy is going to jump into the puddle. What do you think that will do? Do you think that will make the boy and girl happy? Do you think that will make Mother happy? What would you like to say to this boy?

A TIME TO SHARE

1. What is that other boy going to do?

2. What do you think the boy and girl in the puddle will say?

3. Why should that boy not jump like that?

WHAT DO YOU SEE?
How do you know that it has just rained? Point to some things that you would see on a rainy day.

May I Hold It?

My Favorite Thing: A Fluffy Chick

Oh, this little chick feels so soft and fluffy! This girl loves to hold the little chick up to her cheek. Can you feel it? You have done that, haven't you? If you have, you remember how the little chick went *peep, peep.* It was a tiny sound, just as the chick is tiny. But look at that mother hen! She is not tiny now. Do you see how much a chick grows? Look at the girl and then look at Mother. Even a girl grows a lot too. But that's the way God planned things. Wouldn't it be sad if little chicks never grew up? Wouldn't it be sad if little girls never grew up either?

WHAT DO YOU SEE?
How many chicks do you see? What do you see that tells you this is a farm? Why would you not see these things in town?

A TIME TO SHARE
1. *Why is the hen bigger than the chick?*
2. *Why is Mother bigger than the girl?*
3. *Why do you think God planned for us to grow up?*

Yellow Daffodils in My Yard
My Favorite Thing: Daffodils

Now here is something you didn't see last winter. You know it's spring when the daffodils bloom in your backyard. Of course, you will smile when you see their pretty yellow color. Mother smiles because she remembers planting those strange brown bulbs last fall. They didn't look bright yellow. The girl smiles because she helped Mother plant the bulbs. She remembers how dead those bulbs looked. Now she sees beautiful yellow flowers. But how did such pretty yellow flowers come from those old brown bulbs? That's one of God's special gifts to us each spring, isn't it?

WHAT DO YOU SEE?
How many daffodils do you see? What color are they?
Why do you think this is spring?

A TIME TO SHARE
1. *Why are Mother and the girl smiling?*
2. *What did they plant last fall?*
3. *What would you like to say about the daffodils?*

13

Thank You, God

My Favorite Thing: Noah's Big Boat

Have you ever seen a boat like that before? Noah and his family had never seen one like that either. God told Noah to make this boat. He told Noah exactly how to do it. Of course it took Noah a long time. But he wanted to do what God said. If he didn't, he and his family would have drowned in a big flood. Every kind of animal on earth would have drowned too. So Noah made the boat. Then he put many animals and birds on it. Don't you think Noah was glad he did what God said?

A TIME TO SHARE

1. Why did Noah make this big boat?

2. How did it help Noah?

3. Why is Noah saying, "Thank You"?

4. Would you like to thank God for something?

WHAT DO YOU SEE?

Point to the big boat. Do you see what Noah and his family are doing? This is the way people then said, "Thank You, God." Noah wants to thank God that they are safe.

Look What Mother Gave Me

My Favorite Thing: Apple

"Look what Mother gave me today." That's what this boy is saying to his friends. You can see how happy he is. His friends are happy too. They are glad that this boy has a big apple for lunch. That's because they are all good friends. Good friends are glad when one of them has something special. Is that the way you and your friends feel about each other?

A TIME TO SHARE

1. *How many lunches do you see?*
2. *What other food do you see?*
3. *What do you think the boy will do before he eats? Do you?*

WHAT DO YOU SEE?
How do you know this is lunchtime? Why isn't it breakfast? Why isn't it dinner? How do you know this is at school? Why isn't it at the grocery store?

A Windy Day

My Favorite Thing: Wind in the Trees

Oh, what a day to be out in the country! It's a sunny day. But look at that wind. Actually you can't see the wind, can you? You can only see what the wind is doing. But can you feel the wind? Can you know that it is there? These girls know that the wind is blowing. So does that boy who is flying his kite. Do you remember a windy day not long ago? What did you do? Did you see something special?

WHAT DO YOU SEE?
Point to six kinds of things that are blowing in the wind. How would they look if the wind were not blowing? What is the wind doing to the trees?

A TIME TO SHARE
1. *Who sends the wind?*
2. *What are some good things that the wind does?*
3. *Do you like a windy day? Why?*

16

How Will Our Garden Grow?

My Favorite Thing: Seeds

Spring is here! You wouldn't see this family doing these things in the fall. You wouldn't see them out here in the winter, either. But spring is the time to plant a garden. Look at Father. What is he doing? Someone has to dig up the dirt. Mother is helping too. The boy is busy, but what is he doing? Of course the girl wants to help too. Do you think she will help the boy plant some seeds? This family is working together. Do you think that's why they are having so much fun?

WHAT DO YOU SEE?
How do you know this is a garden? What is each person doing? What will they have this summer in their garden?

A TIME TO SHARE
1. *What are these people planting?*
2. *What does the garden need to grow?*
3. *Who sends the rain and sunshine?*
4. *Do you thank God for these things?*

17

Robin Sitting in My Tree

My Favorite Thing: The First Robin

Do you see what I see? It's the first robin we have seen this spring. Look! There is one in the tree outside my window. Do you know what it will do now? Robin will hop on my lawn. Spring is here, isn't it? When Robin comes to stay, spring comes too. Aren't you glad? I am.

WHAT DO YOU SEE?
What do you see in the tree? Who else sees it? Point to each one and tell who it is. Why do you think this is spring?

A TIME TO SHARE
1. *What do you see in the spring that you don't see in the winter?*
2. *What do you like best about spring?*
3. *Will you thank God for it now?*

Walking in the Rain
My Favorite Thing: Umbrella

Do you like to walk in the rain? It's fun if you don't get wet. This girl and her mother are walking in the rain. They have on their good clothes, so they don't want to get wet. That's why Mother brought her umbrella. You can see that she and her girl are glad. Now they can walk in the rain. Now they won't get their good clothes wet. Are you glad for an umbrella on a rainy day?

A TIME TO SHARE

1. Who is holding the umbrella?

2. Are Mother and the girl getting wet? Why not?

3. Are they glad to be together?

WHAT DO YOU SEE?
How do you know that it is raining? What is keeping Mother and the girl from getting wet?

What Are They Making?

My Favorite Thing: Isaac's Well

What are these men making? Have you ever seen men dig a well like this? People don't do that much anymore. Today men drill a hole in the ground. Then they put a pipe into the hole. An electric pump forces the water up through the pipe. But Isaac did not have those kinds of things. He and his men had to dig this well. They had dug another one just like it. But some bad men would not let them use it. Isaac's men wanted to fight. But Isaac thought it was better to dig another well. Do you think he was right?

A TIME TO SHARE

1. *What are these men doing?*
2. *Why didn't they keep the other well?*
3. *What did they do instead of fighting?*
4. *What would you like to say to Isaac?*

WHAT DO YOU SEE?
How is this well different from the place where you get your water? How many men are working on this well? Which one do you think is Isaac?

20

Time to Talk to Jesus

My Favorite Thing: Prayertime at Bedtime

Sometimes you like to go to bed. That's because you're tired. Sometimes you don't like to go to bed. That's because there are fun things to do. And who has enough time to do all the fun things we want to do? This girl thinks bedtime is fun time. She likes to talk to Jesus. Mother and Father like to listen. The girl thanks Jesus for many things. She tells Him how much she loves Him. And she asks Him to help others who need Him. Now you know why she likes prayertime at bedtime.

A TIME TO SHARE

1. *Why are their eyes closed?*
2. *Father is standing, Mother is sitting, and the girl is kneeling. Are they all praying? Can you pray any of these ways?*

WHAT DO YOU SEE?

How do you know this is the girl's bedroom? Who is sharing prayertime with the girl?

A Way to Say I Love You
My Favorite Thing: Wildflowers

This is certainly not a winter day, is it? What time of the year do you think this is? The girl and Father are walking in the woods. Look! There are some new leaves on the trees. And there are some blades of grass poking through the leaves. Puppy is glad he came along. He likes to chase a squirrel on a fine spring day. Now here is something special that the girl has found. Don't you think Father is pleased to get a bouquet of wildflowers from his girl? Don't you think the girl is saying, "I love you, Father"?

A TIME TO SHARE

1. *Why is the girl giving the wildflowers to Father? What is she saying?*
2. *Why is Father happy to get the flowers from his girl? What will he say?*

WHAT DO YOU SEE?
Do you think this is in the city? Why not? Why do you think this is in a woods? How do you know that the girl is happy to be here with Father?

Let's Go Somewhere

My Favorite Thing: Our Speedometer

Do you see who is driving the car today? Father drives some of the time. Mother drives some of the time. Today Mother is home with this boy's sister. That's why he is in the front seat with Father. The boy likes to watch the speedometer. It is more fun to watch it when he is sitting in the front seat. He can see it better. The boy pretends that he is driving the car. He goes slower. Then he goes faster. But he does not go faster than the speed limit. Father does not do that either. Why do you think they do that?

A TIME TO SHARE
1. *Where do you think Father is going?*
2. *What does the boy like to do?*
3. *Why does the boy want to obey the law when he pretends he is driving?*

WHAT DO YOU SEE?
How fast is Father going? He is not going faster than the speed limit. Do you know why he does that? What else is Father doing that he should do?

Wonderful Things to Eat
My Favorite Thing: Peanut Butter and Jam

Do you like peanut butter on a slice of bread? Do you like to spread some jam on it too? Ummm. You can taste the peanut butter and jam now, can't you? And what about the bread? You can taste that too. The girl and boys certainly like the way these things taste! You can see that. Would you like to be here with them now?

WHAT DO YOU SEE?
Where is the bread? How many slices can you find other than the loaf? Point to the peanut butter. And where is the jam? How do they get these things on the bread?

A TIME TO SHARE
1. *Do you like to eat good things?*
2. *Do you like to eat with good friends?*
3. *Why is that more fun than eating alone?*
4. *When do you thank God for your food?*

A New Friend

My Favorite Thing: A Scarecrow

Now here is a friend you don't see every day. You wouldn't meet him in your school playground, would you? You wouldn't see him downtown shopping either. But you would see him here. He's a good friend to have in a garden. This scarecrow won't hoe the garden. He won't plant the seeds. But he will do a special kind of work. Do you know what that is?

A TIME TO SHARE

1. *Who is this new friend?*
2. *What does he do?*
3. *Why do you think they like him?*
4. *What would you say to the scarecrow?*

WHAT DO YOU SEE?

How do you know this is a garden? Point to some things that tell you this. How do you know that these girls and this boy like the scarecrow?

25

A Strange Dream

My Favorite Thing: Jacob's Ladder

This looks like a big escalator at a store. But it isn't. You wouldn't see angels walking up and down an escalator at a store, would you? Jacob had never seen angels anywhere before. How surprised he was to see them on this long stairway! Some people call it a ladder. You would be surprised too, wouldn't you? You would be surprised even if you dreamed it, the way God caused Jacob to do. Now Jacob knows that God is here in this place. He knows now that God will be with him wherever he goes.

WHAT DO YOU SEE?
How many angels do you see? What are they doing? Who is that man at the bottom of the stairway? What is he doing?

A TIME TO SHARE
1. *Who is walking on this stairway?*
2. *Who is here in this place?*
3. *Who will be with Jacob?*

Look What I Found

My Favorite Thing: Grandmother's Trunk

Does your grandmother have an old trunk in her attic? This grandmother does. It is filled with exciting surprises for the boy and girl. Look! Do you see what the girl has found? Who do you think wore that hat before it was put into the trunk? Do you see what the boy found? It's a picture of some-one. But whose picture is it? Would you like to guess? Grandmother's trunk is a special place. That's because it has all these exciting surprises. What do you think the boy and girl will find next?

WHAT DO YOU SEE?
Do you think Grandmother cares if the boy and girl are looking in the trunk? How do you know? What else do you see in the attic?

A TIME TO SHARE
1. *Whose attic is this?*
2. *Why is Grandmother's trunk fun?*
3. *Why isn't Grandmother angry?*
4. *Do you think they love each other?*

What's Outside My Window?

My Favorite Thing: A Bird's Nest

Oh, look! Do you see what I see outside my window? A bird has come to stay at our house. It has made its house outside my window. Father and I call it a nest. You do too, don't you? Do you know what that bird put into its nest? Do you know how the baby birds got there?

A TIME TO SHARE

1. *Why is the boy so excited?*
2. *What happened in this nest?*
3. *Who else is watching the bird besides Father and the boy?*

WHAT DO YOU SEE?

What do you see in the boy's room? Which of these things would you probably not see in a girl's room? Why not?

I Love You, Kitty

My Favorite Thing: My Kitty

Now here's a happy picture. You can see that Father is happy. That's because the girl is happy. Do you know why she is happy? That's because Kitty is happy. But why is Kitty happy? Is that because the girl loves her? Do you suppose we are happiest when we know that someone special loves us?

A TIME TO SHARE

1. Do you think the girl loves Kitty?

2. How do you know?

3. Do you think Father loves the girl?

4. Do you think Jesus loves them all?

WHAT DO YOU SEE?

How many frowns do you see? How many happy faces do you see?

29

Do You See What I See?

My Favorite Thing: A Big Moth

Look at that big, beautiful moth! Have you ever seen such a big one? This boy hasn't. That's why he is calling to his mother and father. "Come and see what I see!" he is telling them. He wants to share what he has found. When you find something wonderful, do you like to share it with someone else? Perhaps that is why you like to tell others about Jesus. Is it?

A TIME TO SHARE

1. *What is the boy pointing to?*
2. *Why is he calling Mother and Father?*
3. *Why should we share something wonderful that we have found?*

WHAT DO YOU SEE?

How do you know this family is in the woods? Point to some things that tell you. Do you think this is a spring day or a winter day? How do you know?

One Hundred Buttons

My Favorite Thing: Buttons

Do you know what Mother is doing? This boy knows. She is doing it for him, isn't she? Sewing buttons on clothing is not easy. But Mother knows how. The boy is glad that she does. Who else would do it? The boy could not do it. And Father is at work. But Mother is here. And Mother thinks it is special fun to do this for her boy. Aren't you glad for all the special things Mother does for you?

A TIME TO SHARE

1. What is Mother doing?

2. Name all the things that Mother does for you. How many can you name?

3. Would you like to thank her now?

WHAT DO YOU SEE?
How many buttons can you count? Do you suppose there are 100 buttons in that jar? Name each thing Mother will use to sew on that button.

It's Raining

My Favorite Thing: Rain

Here is a boy who is glad to be inside today. Do you see why? It's fun to watch the raindrops come down. It's fun to see some raindrops run down the windowpane. But it's more fun when you're inside, looking out. God gives us rain for special reasons. Can you think of some good things the rain does for us?

WHAT DO YOU SEE?
How do you know it is raining? What would the boy have to put on if he went outside now?

A TIME TO SHARE
1. *Who sends the rain?*
2. *What would happen if it did not rain?*
3. *Would you like to thank God for rain?*

Jesus Is Alive!

My Favorite Thing: The Stone that Rolled Away

That's a big stone! You can see that someone has worked hard to make it round. That's so the stone can roll back and forth. Now you can see what is behind the stone. It is a cave. That's where Jesus was buried. But Jesus didn't stay there very long. You know what happened. He came back to life. Then that big stone was rolled back. Jesus came out of the cave. He was alive! He was not dead now. He would never die again. That's because He is God's Son. Aren't you glad Jesus is alive!

WHAT DO YOU SEE?
Do you see the stone? Do you see the place where it rolls back and forth? Do you see the cave behind the stone?

A TIME TO SHARE
1. *Who was in this cave?*
2. *Why was this stone rolled away?*
3. *Where is Jesus now?*
4. *Why are you glad that He is alive?*

Look at All Those Eggs!

My Favorite Thing: An Egg

Look at all those eggs! It must be Easter. You can see what Mother and her boy and girl are doing. Do you do this at Easter? It's fun to dye eggs. It's fun to eat them too. Sometimes mother chickens get to keep their eggs. They sit on them until the eggs are ready to hatch. Then the shell breaks open and a baby chick comes out.

WHAT DO YOU SEE?
How many eggs can you count? What colors do you see? Do you see something that lays eggs? Point to them.

A TIME TO SHARE
1. *What are these people doing?*
2. *Why do you think this is fun?*
3. *What would you say if you were here?*

Where Are We Going?

My Favorite Thing: A Road Map

Now here's a family that's ready to go somewhere. You can see their car is ready. And the picnic lunch is almost ready. Mother is putting in the last things. But where are they going? And what is the best way to get there? Father knows where to find the way. It's called a road map. Don't you think he and the boy are wise to look at it carefully? What could happen if they don't?

A TIME TO SHARE

1. *How will the road map help?*
2. *Why does this family like a picnic?*
3. *Why do you like a picnic?*

WHAT DO YOU SEE?

Can you find the road map? What will it tell Father? Do you see the robin in the tree? It goes places too, but it never needs a road map. God tells it where to go.

Thank You for My Eyes

My Favorite Thing: My Eyes

I have two eyes. How many do you have? Puppy has two eyes too! But Father teases me. He says he has four eyes. Do you know what he means? You can see Father sitting there in his chair. He is reading his newspaper. But he cannot read it without some help. That's why he says he has four eyes. Some of my friends at school have glasses too. They need their glasses to read better. I'm glad for my eyes. They help me see many wonderful things. Point to some things you see because you have good eyes.

WHAT DO YOU SEE?
How many eyes do you see in this picture? Point to each one. How many eyes do the boy, his reflection, Father, and the puppy have altogether?

A TIME TO SHARE
1. *What do you see now with your eyes?*
2. *Close your eyes. How would it feel not to see?*
3. *Do you thank God for your eyes?*

36

My Favorite

My Favorite Thing: My Teddy Bear

Here is a girl with lots of bedtime friends. She loves each one of them. But she loves one of them more than the others. Can you guess which one that is? Mother knows. She makes sure the girl has her teddy bear at bedtime. What do you think the girl would do if she could not find her teddy bear? What would you do?

A TIME TO SHARE

1. *What does the girl have with her?*
2. *Why does she have them?*
3. *What stuffed animals do you have?*
4. *Which do you like best? Why?*

WHAT DO YOU SEE?
How many stuffed animals does this girl have with her? Point to each one and tell which kind of animal it is.

Will You Come to My Party?

My Favorite Thing: My Birthday Cake

There it is, with candles already lit. Can you count the candles? That's how old the boy is. Now he is going to blow on those candles. That's the part that's fun! Watch them go out! What would a birthday be without a birthday cake?

WHAT DO YOU SEE?
How many things do you see that tell you this is a birthday party? Can you name each one? How many boys are at this party?

A TIME TO SHARE
1. *Why should birthdays be happy times? Are these boys happy?*
2. *Why is that one boy not happy?*
3. *What do you do on your birthday?*

Something Beautiful
My Favorite Thing: Joseph's Coat

This young man is glad for his beautiful coat. You can see that, can't you? But you wouldn't be glad for Joseph's coat, would you? You and your friends do not dress like that. In Bible days, Joseph and his friends dressed this way. Anyone was glad for a beautiful new coat. But not many young men got a coat as nice as this. It was better than others. That's because Joseph's father wanted to tell Joseph how much he loved him. He wanted to tell others that he loved Joseph more than any other son.

WHAT DO YOU SEE?
How is this coat different from the clothing you wear? How is Joseph's tent-home different from your house?

A TIME TO SHARE
1. *Why is Joseph so happy?*
2. *What does Joseph's coat tell others?*
3. *Are you glad when someone likes you?*
4. *Do you like to get beautiful gifts?*

Busy Fingers

My Favorite Thing: My Fingers

What a busy family! Do you see Father at his desk? What is he doing? Is he writing with his feet? Is he doing this with his nose? What does he use to hold the pen? Do you see Mother? She is busy too. What is she doing? Is she knitting with her toes? What is she using? The girl is having fun too. She is taking piano lessons. Her teacher helps her do wonderful things with her fingers. The boy does wonderful things with his fingers too. Puppy thinks so now. Don't you think these people are all glad for their busy fingers?

WHAT DO YOU SEE?
How many fingers do these people have? How many does each person have? Why doesn't Puppy have fingers? What does Puppy have instead?

A TIME TO SHARE
1. *What can you do with your fingers?*
2. *Why do you think God gave fingers?*
3. *What can you do that Puppy can't?*
4. *Have you thanked God for fingers?*

Look What I'm Doing

My Favorite Thing: My Toothbrush

When do you brush your teeth? Do you do it when you get up in the morning? Do you do it when you go to bed? Do you do it some other time? It feels good to brush that furry stuff from our teeth, doesn't it? And toothpaste tastes good too. Do you like that minty taste? This girl does. Kitty is watching the girl brush her teeth. But Kitty never needs to do that. God gave Kitty her own way to keep her teeth clean. God knows that Kitty could not brush her teeth, doesn't He?

WHAT DO YOU SEE?
What room is this? Point to some things that you have in your bathroom. How do you use each one?

A TIME TO SHARE
1. *What is the girl doing? Why?*
2. *Why isn't Kitty doing this?*
3. *Why do you brush your teeth?*

Listen to My Music
My Favorite Thing: A Xylophone

Now here is something you would like to do. This girl is having fun. When she hits the right keys, she plays music. The boy is waiting. He would like to do that too. The dog thinks it is fun to hear, but he would rather do something that dogs like to do. What do you think that would be? Do you have a xylophone? What can you play on it?

WHAT DO YOU SEE?
How many keys do you see on the xylophone? How does the girl make music on it?

A TIME TO SHARE
1. *What is the girl doing?*
2. *Do you think you could play "Jesus Loves Me" on this?*
3. *Pretend that you are doing this.*

Look at This Happy Family

My Favorite Thing: Our New Baby

What a special day this is! The boy and girl have a new baby sister. This is the first time they have seen her. The nurse is happy to show them their new baby sister. Of course Father is happy too. You can see that, can't you? Mother is happy, but she can't be with them now. She is in a bed inside the hospital. But she will be home soon. Then the boy and girl can hold their baby sister. That will be even more special, won't it? They will help Mother and Father take care of her. Would you like to hold this baby?

A TIME TO SHARE

1. Why is Father happy?

2. Why are the boy and girl happy?

3. Do you think they love this baby?

4. Why should we love a new baby?

WHAT DO YOU SEE?
Where is this? How do you know? Who are those two ladies on the other side of the window? Can you point to the place where the babies sleep?

The Sun Is Smiling

My Favorite Thing: My Bed

"Good morning!" That's Mother peeking around the corner. It's time to get up. But this girl wants to stay in her bed. You know how she feels, don't you? Your bed is the warmest, coziest, snuggliest place of all. It's time to get up. But your nice cozy bed says, "Stay here a little longer." And Mother says, "The sun is smiling. It's waiting for you." What should you do?

A TIME TO SHARE

1. *Why do you like your bed?*
2. *How long do you sleep each night?*
3. *Who watches over you while you sleep?*
4. *What should you say to Him?*

WHAT DO YOU SEE?
What time is it? How do you know it is time to get up? Which room is this? How do you know?

44

A Basket for the Baby

My Favorite Thing: Baby Moses' Basket

Look! Do you see that basket on the river? Baby Moses was in that basket. His mother put him there. She wanted to hide her baby from the wicked king. But look who found him! The princess is holding Baby Moses close to her. She wants to keep him. Now the king will not hurt him. Aren't you glad that Baby Moses is safe? Now you know that God takes care of us.

A TIME TO SHARE

1. *Who wanted to hurt Baby Moses?*
2. *Where did his mother hide him?*
3. *Why is he safe now?*
4. *Do you thank God when He helps you?*

WHAT DO YOU SEE?

Where is Baby Moses' basket? What is in it? What was in it? Do you think the princess is rich or poor? Why?

Look What Came Today!
My Favorite Thing: A Birthday Card

Are you excited when you get something special in the mail? This girl is! Father has just brought it in from the mailbox. The girl knows it's a birthday card because today is her birthday. She knows it is from someone special. Do you think it is from Grandfather and Grandmother? They will say some good things to the girl. They will say "happy birthday." They will also say "we love you." Don't you think the girl will say "I love you too" when she reads that?

WHAT DO YOU SEE?
Whose pictures do you see on the wall? Why do you think that's who they are? Can you find the mailbox? Why is the mailbox important to these people?

A TIME TO SHARE
1. *What is Father holding in his hand?*
2. *Why does this make the girl happy?*
3. *How do you feel when you get a birthday card from someone special?*

Look at Me!

My Favorite Things: Grown-up Clothes

Look at that girl! What is she doing? Mother thinks it is funny to see the girl in her clothes. Do you think it is funny too? If you're a girl you probably like to dress up in Mother's clothes and pretend to be someone else. Or if you're a boy you may like to put on Father's hat or cap. It's fun to pretend that we're grown up. But then it's fun to be a boy or girl again, isn't it? You really wouldn't want to do all that Mother or Father does today, would you? By the way, don't forget to thank them for all they do for you.

WHAT DO YOU SEE?
Why do you think those are Mother's clothes on the girl? Why do you think Mother is smiling?

A TIME TO SHARE
1. *Why is it fun to pretend?*
2. *Would you want to be a grown-up today?*
3. *What are some things you want to do before you become a grown-up?*

A Special Time

My Favorite Thing: Bible-time at Dinnertime

Dinner is over and now it is time to do something else. This family is doing something that your family may like to do. Can you see what they are doing? Father is reading from a special Book. The boy and Mother are listening to what Father reads. The boy likes to hear Father read from the Bible. He can listen to his Father's voice. But he can also hear what God is saying in His Book. Don't you think Bible-time at dinnertime can be a special time?

WHAT DO YOU SEE?

What time is it? Why do you think this is evening and not morning? How can you tell that dinner is over, not just beginning?

A TIME TO SHARE

1. *What is Father doing?*
2. *What are the boy and Mother doing?*
3. *Why does the boy listen now?*
4. *Why should we read the Bible?*

Lunchtime!

My Favorite Thing: My Lunch Box

Look at that clock on the wall! Do you see what time it is? Is this the middle of the night? Or is it the middle of the day? You can see that it is lunchtime. Do you see the lunch boxes? And do you see what is in the lunch boxes? This morning these boys and girls did not think their lunch boxes were so important. But now each lunch box is one of their favorite things. Do you know why?

A TIME TO SHARE

1. *What are these boys and girls doing?*
2. *What do you think they did before they began to eat their lunch?*
3. *What do you do before eating? Why?*

WHAT DO YOU SEE?
What do you see in the lunch boxes? Why would you not see these things at the breakfast table?

Time for Dessert

My Favorite Thing: Cherry Pie

Dinner is over and it's time for dessert. That's a happy time for this boy. You can see that he likes the dessert Mother has made for them tonight. Cherry pie is a favorite thing for this boy. Tonight Father is putting something else on the cherry pie. After Mother cuts the pie, Father puts some ice cream on it. Now you know why the boy looks so happy. What would taste better right now than cherry pie and ice cream?

A TIME TO SHARE

1. *What is this family doing?*
2. *Why do you like some food better than other food?*
3. *What dessert do you like best?*

WHAT DO YOU SEE?

Who is cutting the pie? Who is putting the ice cream on it? Who will eat the pie and ice cream? Is that why they all look so happy?

Where Are You Going So Fast?

My Favorite Thing: A Chariot

You wouldn't see this thing going down your street, would you? People in your town drive cars or trucks or vans. But this man did not have any of those. Nobody then had those things. He was glad to have a chariot. Only a very important person had one. Sometimes a king had many chariots. He had soldiers drive them into a battle. It was better fighting in a chariot. Do you suppose that's what this man is doing?

A TIME TO SHARE

1. *How is a chariot different from your car?*
2. *How is this man different from your father? Would you want your father to do this? Would you want to do this?*

WHAT DO YOU SEE?

How many arrows can you find? Can you find 10? What else do you see that you do not see around your house?

51

Ummm. That Smells Good!

My Favorite Thing: My Nose

Have you ever looked at your nose? You have to see it in a mirror, don't you? It's very hard to see your nose unless you look in a mirror. God put it where it would not keep your eyes from seeing. God made your nose for something important. What do you do with it? How would dinnertime be different without it? How would springtime be without it? Do you remember to thank God for your nose? Why not do that now?

A TIME TO SHARE

1. *How many things can you smell? Make a list of all the things you think of.*
2. *Which of these things don't you like to smell? Which do you like to smell?*

WHAT DO YOU SEE?
What do you think the girl smells now? What will she smell tonight when Mother gets dinner?

Having Fun Together

My Favorite Thing: Marbles

You can see those two boys are having fun, can't you? They are playing with some marbles. But look at that other boy. He is not having fun. You can see that. Do you think he is angry at the other boys? What else could be the matter? Do you think Jesus is more pleased when we have fun together, or when we are angry at one another?

A TIME TO SHARE

1. Do you like to play games with friends?

2. Why is that better than fighting?

3. Why is Jesus pleased when you have fun with your friends or family?

WHAT DO YOU SEE?

How many marbles do you see? Don't forget the one in the boy's hand. What else do you see that the boys could play with?

Time to Get Up
My Favorite Thing: My Pillow

It's time to get up! But this girl would rather stay in bed. Have you ever felt that way? Sometimes bed feels so warm and cozy. Of course there is something about a favorite pillow too. A pillow is like a friend. This girl takes her pillow with her when she stays at a friend's house. She even takes it with her when she goes with her family on a trip. Do you? Now you know why it's hard to get up. Who wants to leave a warm, cozy bed and a favorite pillow. But it's time to get up! Hurry! Breakfast is waiting.

WHAT DO YOU SEE?
Where is the girl's pillow? What else do you see in her room? What do you see that you have in your room? What do you see that you don't have?

A TIME TO SHARE
1. *Who has come to wake up this girl?*
2. *Why doesn't the girl want to get up?*
3. *Why does she like her pillow?*
4. *Why do you like your pillow?*

54

Will You Buy a Treat for Me?

My Favorite Thing: Mother's Purse

Oh, look! Do you see all that wonderful candy? There's some peppermint. And here's some chocolate. And do you see the gumdrops? This boy and girl want some of the candy. Mother is happy to get them some today. She does not buy candy for them often. She does not think they should have much candy. But today is a special day. So Mother opens her purse. She reaches in. Now the girl knows Mother will buy some candy. The boy can almost taste it. Mother's purse is special. It helps the boy and girl get candy. It helps them get other things too.

A TIME TO SHARE

1. What do the boy and girl want?

2. Who can buy it for them?

3. Why do you think she will?

4. Why is Mother's purse so special?

WHAT DO YOU SEE?
How many kinds of candy can you find? You may need to guess at some of them. Do you see Mother's purse? What do you think is in it? Why is money important?

God Sends Good Food

My Favorite Thing: Manna

These people were hungry. They had no food to eat. You can see why. This is not a garden. It is not an orchard. It is called a wilderness. That's because nothing much grows here. And there are no animals to hunt or fish either. But God has sent some special food for these people. You can see it on the ground. It is manna. Would you like this for dinner tonight? Would you like it for dinner every night this year? That's the way it was for these people. But they were glad that God sent good food. It was all they had.

WHAT DO YOU SEE?
Point to the manna. How do you know it is good to eat? What is the girl putting her manna in? Where will she take her basket when it is full?

A TIME TO SHARE
1. *Who sent this manna?*
2. *Why did God send it?*
3. *What do you think these people said to God then? What would you say?*

56

Our Happy Family

My Favorite Thing: A Favorite Book

Can you guess why Father is smiling? He should smile, shouldn't he? He is looking at two happy people. Do you know who they are? Mother is happy because she can read a favorite book to her girl. There's something warm and wonderful about that. The girl is happy because she loves to have Mother read her favorite book to her. And Father is happy because he sees Mother and the girl happy. Of course Kitty is happy too. Are you happy when you see things like this?

WHAT DO YOU SEE?

How many smiles do you see? How many frowns do you see? Which person is making the others happy? What do Mother and the girl have in their hands?

A TIME TO SHARE

1. *What are Mother and the girl doing?*
2. *Why does this make each happy?*
3. *What book do you think this is?*
4. *Why should we read the Bible?*

57

Will You Share My Stars?

My Favorite Thing: Stars through My Window

Oh, look! Do you see those beautiful stars through the window? This girl sees them. She wants Mother to see them too. It's fun to share beautiful things with someone we love, isn't it? That's why the girl wants Mother to see them. These stars are too beautiful to keep. We like to give away things like that if we can. Can you think of other beautiful things you would like to share?

WHAT DO YOU SEE?
Which room is this? Is it Mother's bedroom? Is it the girl's bedroom? Point to some things that tell you which room it is.

A TIME TO SHARE
1. *How do you know this is night?*
2. *What does the girl see?*
3. *Why does she want Mother to see them?*
4. *Why do you like to share good things?*

Rings on Your Fingers
My Favorite Thing: Mother's Rings

Mother has something special on her finger. Do you know what it is? This girl knows. She likes to look at Mother's rings. One ring has a big diamond on it. The other has some little diamonds. Mother smiles when she looks at her rings. She is glad that Father gave them to her. She is glad that she is married to Father. The girl is glad too. She is especially glad that Mother and Father love each other. Don't you think she should be glad about that?

WHAT DO YOU SEE?
What do you see on Mother's hand? Is Mother smiling or frowning? Is the girl smiling or frowning? They both like to look at Mother's rings, don't they?

A TIME TO SHARE
1. *Who gave Mother the rings? Why?*
2. *Why is Mother happy?*
3. *Why is the girl happy?*
4. *What would you like to say to them?*

Something Sweet
My Favorite Thing: Peppermint

Would you like to visit this store? These boys and this girl like to come here. You can see why. But Mother and Father won't let them come too often. They know that too much candy isn't good for anyone. Today is a special day. It's a day for peppermint. It could be chocolate. Or it could be gumdrops. But today each person wants a stick of peppermint. Is today a peppermint day for you?

WHAT DO YOU SEE?
What kind of store is this? How do you know? Can you point to some different kinds of candy? How do they taste?

A TIME TO SHARE
1. *What are the children buying?*
2. *Is it sweet or sour? What makes it that way?*
3. *What would you say if you were here?*

A Special Tent

My Favorite Thing: God's Tent-House

Do you see that tent? It is a special kind of tent. God told His people to make it. He even told them how to make it. That's because the people would use it for God's house. The people made this tent and its furniture from the best that they had. They used gold, silver, and precious jewels. God's house would be the very best. It would be the kind of place that would please God. Don't you think that's the way it should be?

A TIME TO SHARE

1. What is this tent?

2. Why is it made with beautiful things?

3. How is it different from your church?

WHAT DO YOU SEE?
Find the big bowl. Priests washed in it. It was a way to keep clean for God. Do you see the meat burning? That was a way the people told God they were sorry for their sins.

Going to God's House

My Favorite Thing: Our Church

Where is this family going? Are they going to the store? Are they going to school? You can see that they are going to church, can't you? They like to go to church together. They like to take their Bibles. Then they can know what God is saying to them. Can you think of other things they will do at church today?

A TIME TO SHARE

1. Why are these people smiling?

2. What will they do this morning?

3. What do you learn at church and Sunday School?

WHAT DO YOU SEE?

How many Bibles do you see? What do you see that tells you this is a church?

Grandfather's Chair

My Favorite Thing: A Rocking Chair

This boy has found something that he likes very much. Back and forth, back and forth, the boy rocks in that big rocking chair. You can see that it is not his own chair. It belongs to someone he loves very much. Do you know who that is? You can see him in the picture. The boy is staying at Grandfather's house. Grandfather has many things that the boy does not have. This rocking chair is one of them. Why do you suppose this rocking chair is one of the boy's favorite things?

A TIME TO SHARE

1. *What is the boy sitting in?*
2. *What do you do with a rocking chair?*
3. *What do you think the boy is thinking?*
4. *What would you say if you were here?*

WHAT DO YOU SEE?
Point to four things that Grandfather has at his house. Which person is Grandfather? Point to him.

Will You Fix My Bike?

My Favorite Thing: Father's Tool Chest

Here's Father, trying to fix his boy's bike. You can see what's wrong. That bolt needs to be tighter. Father knows what tool will do the job. That's why he is using it. But the boy teases him. You can see what he is holding. What would you say if you were Father?

WHAT DO YOU SEE?
Can you name the two tools? Which one is the boy holding? Which is Father holding? What other tools do you think are in Father's tool chest?

A TIME TO SHARE
1. *What is Father doing?*
2. *What should the boy say when Father has finished?*
3. *Why should he say that?*

64

Where Do We Live?

My Favorite Thing: A Globe

Where do we live? That's what these boys are asking. Of course they know where to find their houses down the street. They can walk to their school, or their church, or downtown. But where is our country on this globe? And where is our town? The boys will find these things, won't they? But as they look they see other countries too. Look! There is Japan and Denmark and Nigeria. Each of those countries has boys and girls, mothers and fathers. And Jesus loves each person there, just as He loves these boys. Aren't you glad some people are telling others about Jesus?

A TIME TO SHARE

1. *Does Jesus love everyone?*

2. *Did He die for everyone?*

3. *Why should we tell everyone about Him?*

WHAT DO YOU SEE?

What do you see on the wall? What does this tell you about people of other lands? What does the globe remind you about people of other lands?

Something to Share
My Favorite Thing: That Big Bunch of Grapes

That bunch of grapes is really big, isn't it? It's bigger than any other bunch of grapes you have seen. It is bigger than any bunch of grapes these men had seen too. But these men had never been to Canaan before. That's where they found these grapes. They wanted their friends to see what they had found. So they brought the grapes home with them. When you find something special, don't you like to share it with friends and family? Most of us do!

WHAT DO YOU SEE?
How are these men carrying the grapes? Why do they have to carry them on a pole? Why aren't these men dressed in jeans or a suit?

A TIME TO SHARE
1. *Where are the men taking these grapes?*
2. *What will they do with them?*
3. *When you find something special, what do you like to do with it? Why?*

Thank You, Mother

My Favorite Thing: A Bandage

You know that this boy hurt himself. Was it a cut? Or did he pinch his finger in the door? It could be either. But it hurts. You know how the boy feels, don't you? You've cut your finger or pinched it in the door, haven't you? What did you do then? Did you ask Mother to put a bandage on it? The bandage felt good. But Mother's warm smile felt good too. Weren't you glad that Mother put on the bandage? You knew everything would be all right. It was too.

WHAT DO YOU SEE?
Why do you think the boy hurts? What do you see that tells you this? What is Mother putting on his finger?

A TIME TO SHARE
1. *What do you think Mother is saying to the boy?*
2. *What do you think the boy is saying to Mother?*

Mother's Helper

My Favorite Thing: A Grocery Cart

This girl likes to go grocery shopping with Mother. Do you? Mother is glad the girl is with her. You can see what a good helper she is. The girl likes to push the grocery cart for Mother. Of course when the cart gets too full, Mother helps her helper. Do you like to help Mother push the grocery cart? Do you like to be Mother's helper? Of course you don't mind when Mother helps her helper, do you?

A TIME TO SHARE

1. What is Mother doing?

2. What is the girl doing?

3. Why do you like to help Mother?

4. Why does this please Jesus?

WHAT DO YOU SEE?

What kind of store is this? What do you see that tells you that? Would you see these things at a shoe store? Would you see them at a clothing store? Why not?

I'm Hungry

My Favorite Thing: A Hot Dog with Everything

Ummmm! There are times when a hot dog with everything tastes special. This is one of those times. Father and the boy are on a long walk. Do you think they are at the zoo? Or could they be in the park? Perhaps they could be at a place with a merry-go-round and other rides. It must be *one* of these. That hot dog wouldn't taste as good for Sunday dinner at home, would it? But here it's a special treat. You can see that Father is going to have one too. Would you like a hot dog with everything? What would you say if Father bought you one?

A TIME TO SHARE

1. *What are Father and the boy doing?*
2. *Why are they having so much fun?*
3. *Why do hot dogs taste better here than for Sunday dinner?*

WHAT DO YOU SEE?

What do you think is on the hot dog? Point to the buns. Can you find the catsup? What about the mustard? Do you suppose there is pickle relish too?

Something Beautiful to Share

My Favorite Thing: A Rainbow

Look! Do you see what I see up in the sky? It is something beautiful, with many colors. This boy sees it. He wants to share this beautiful rainbow with his friends. "Do you see it?" he asks them. Do you think they do? Of course they do. They are glad their friend saw it. They are glad he shared this beautiful rainbow with them. Do you like to share beautiful things you see with your friends?

WHAT DO YOU SEE?
What do you see these friends wearing? What kind of a day has this been? Was it snowing? Was it raining?

A TIME TO SHARE
1. *What does the boy see?*
2. *Why is he pointing to the rainbow?*
3. *Why do you like to share beautiful things with friends or family?*

Look at That Bush!

My Favorite Thing: The Burning Bush

Have you ever seen a bush like that? You can see that it is burning. Moses sees it too. But the bush keeps on burning. It does not burn up. Moses had never seen anything like that before. He had never heard God talk from a bush before either. But that is what he is hearing now. Do you see Moses? He is listening carefully. He hears God tell him what to do. Don't you think it is a good idea to say yes when God tells us what to do? That's what Moses did.

A TIME TO SHARE

1. *What did God tell Moses?*
2. *What did Moses tell God?*
3. *What would you have said?*

WHAT DO YOU SEE?
Point to the bush. What is different from most bushes? Point to Moses. What is he doing? Why is he doing this?

What Is That Up There?

My Favorite Thing: The Man on the Moon

Do you see what that boy sees? It's fun to look at the big full moon, isn't it? Sometimes the boy thinks he sees a face on the moon. Someone told him, "It's the man on the moon." You've heard of that, haven't you? Of course it isn't really a face. And it isn't really a man on the moon, is it? But it is fun to pretend. Do you like to pretend like this?

A TIME TO SHARE

1. *What could this boy be thinking?*
2. *What would you like to say to him?*
3. *Are you glad God made the moon? Why?*
4. *What else do you see at night?*

WHAT DO YOU SEE?

What time of day is this? Is it noon? Is it morning? Why not? What do you think Mother is doing now?

Dinnertime at the Barn

My Favorite Thing: Grandfather's Barn

It's dinnertime at Grandfather's barn. But who is eating? Is it Grandfather? Is it the boy? Is it the girl? Of course not. People don't eat this kind of dinner, do they? Do you see what Grandfather is doing? He is feeding the cow. But who else is having dinner? Do you see them? What do you think they are eating? It's fun for the boy and girl to help Grandfather. It's fun when it's dinnertime at Grandfather's barn.

A TIME TO SHARE

1. *Who made these animals?*
2. *How are they different?*
3. *Did God make their food?*
4. *How are you different from them?*

WHAT DO YOU SEE?
Point to each animal in the barn. Point to each thing an animal can eat. Do chickens eat straw? Do cows peck grain from the floor? Why not?

Thank You for Ice Cream
My Favorite Thing: An Ice Cream Cone

How would you like an ice cream cone like that? You can see that the boy is happy to get it. Look at him reach for it. Father wants one too. But he will get this one for the boy first. Then he will buy one for himself. Father and the boy could have bought one of those other things pictured on the wall. But they want to walk down the street, eating their ice cream cones. Doesn't that sound like fun? The boy is glad Father is with him.

WHAT DO YOU SEE?
Why do you think this is a summer day, and not a winter day? What kind of store is this? Is it a grocery store? Is it a hardware store? Why not?

A TIME TO SHARE
1. *Which flavors of ice cream do you think are on the cone?*
2. *Which flavors do you like best?*
3. *Will the boy thank Father?*
4. *Do you thank Father and Mother often?*

Red or Yellow?

My Favorite Thing: A Balloon

Look! What is that man holding? The man is glad he can sell balloons. It makes boys and girls happy. You can see that. This boy is excited. He wants a balloon. "Red or yellow? Blue or green?" asks the man. The boy points to the color he wants. Which one do you think that is?

A TIME TO SHARE

1. Who will pay for this balloon?

2. How do you know?

3. Why do you think Father is doing this?

4. What should the boy say?

WHAT DO YOU SEE?

How many balloons do you see? Can you name each color? What is that other boy doing? Why? Do you think he was careless?

What Did You Say?
My Favorite Thing: Balaam's Donkey

Have you ever heard a donkey talk? Balaam didn't think a donkey could talk. But God wanted to tell Balaam something. So God caused the donkey to speak. Balaam knew that the donkey was really speaking God's words. He listened. You would too, wouldn't you? Then Balaam said he would do what God wanted.

WHAT DO YOU SEE?
What is Balaam riding? What does he have in his hand? What do you think he does with that stick? What does he have in his other hand? Why?

A TIME TO SHARE
1. *Who talked to Balaam?*
2. *What did He tell him?*
3. *What did Balaam do then?*
4. *Do you like to do what God says? Why?*

Do You See the Birds?

My Favorite Thing: Birds

Do you see those birds? How many do you see? Don't forget the one in the tree. What do you think that bird is doing? Look at the one on the post. What is it doing? Now here comes another bird. What is it doing? Father is telling the boy and girl about the bird that is flying. What do you think he is saying? Do you think he is telling them about the other thing that is flying? This boy and girl like to watch birds fly. It reminds them of the many wonderful things God does for His friends.

WHAT DO YOU SEE?
What do you see that would like to catch these birds? Do you think she will? Who would stop her?

A TIME TO SHARE
1. *Who teaches birds to fly?*
2. *What else does He do for them?*
3. *What does God do for you?*

Do You See the Moon?

My Favorite Thing: The Moon Rising

Now there is something we all like to see. Have you ever watched a full moon rising? Have you seen it rise behind some pine trees? Was that when you and your family were camping? That's what this family sees. Do you see the campfire? Do you smell the pine trees? Do you smell the wood smoke from the fire? Do you see the full moon? Don't you think this is a wonderful time to thank God for His beautiful world?

WHAT DO YOU SEE?
What do you see that tells you this is a campground in the woods? Point to some things that you like. Why do you like them?

A TIME TO SHARE
1. *What is this family doing?*
2. *What do they see?*
3. *What do you think they are saying?*
4. *What would you say if you saw this?*

78

A Summer Treat

My Favorite Thing: Ripe Watermelon

One for you and one for me. That's what Father says when he cuts ripe watermelon on a summer day. Do you see him? He has cut a piece for the boy. He has cut another for the girl. But there are two more pieces on the plate. Who are those for? Even Puppy wants a piece. Who wouldn't want a piece of ripe watermelon on a hot summer day? Would you?

A TIME TO SHARE

1. What is Father cutting?

2. What color is ripe watermelon?

3. Does it grow on a tree? Where?

4. Do you think they prayed first?

WHAT DO YOU SEE?
How many pieces of watermelon has Father cut? Point to each one. What else will this family have for lunch? How many glasses do you see?

Down We Go!

My Favorite Thing: My Slide

Down we go! Oh, what fun to go down the slide. Of course we must climb up the ladder again. But Mother will help us up. And then down we go again. Father is there. He will catch us. I know he will not let us get hurt. Father always takes care of us. Mother takes care of us too. That's the way it should be, isn't it?

A TIME TO SHARE
1. *What is the boy doing?*
2. *What is the girl doing?*
3. *What are Mother and Father doing?*
4. *Why is this a happy family?*

WHAT DO YOU SEE?
Who is helping the boy as he comes down the slide?
Who is helping the girl as she goes up the ladder?
Why do the boy and girl feel better when Mother and Father are there?

A Storm Is Coming

My Favorite Thing: A Storm

Oh, my! Look at those ponies run. They know that a storm is coming. Father is telling them to hurry. The boy is telling them to hurry too. But they do not need to say that. The ponies are running to get into the barn, aren't they? Listen! Do you hear the thunder? Look! Do you see the lightning? And do you feel the wind blowing on your face? This boy likes to hear the thunder. He likes to see the lightning. He likes to feel the wind. He is not afraid. That's because Father is with him. Do you feel that way too?

A TIME TO SHARE

1. Why isn't the boy afraid?

2. Why isn't Father afraid? Who is with him?

3. Who is with you during a storm?

WHAT DO YOU SEE?
How do you know that a storm is coming? Point to three things that tell you so.

Let's Go for a Walk

My Favorite Thing: Summer Clouds

Look! Do you see what I see up in the sky? Do you see those big puffy white things? Are they trees? Are they birds? Of course not. But what are they? This girl knows what they are. She likes to look at the puffy white clouds. She likes to watch them float across the sky. Sometimes she thinks she sees faces or shapes in the clouds. Do you ever do that? Father and the girl talk about the white clouds. They talk about the pretend things they see. And they talk about the way God made this beautiful world. The girl is glad God made the white clouds. She is glad God made the other beautiful things they see today. Are you? Do you thank Him for them?

WHAT DO YOU SEE?

Where are Father and the girl? Are they on a city street? Are they in your neighborhood? Point to some things that tell you this is in the country.

A TIME TO SHARE

1. *What are these people doing?*
2. *Do you like to walk with Father or Mother? What do you talk about?*
3. *Would you like to thank God for summer clouds?*

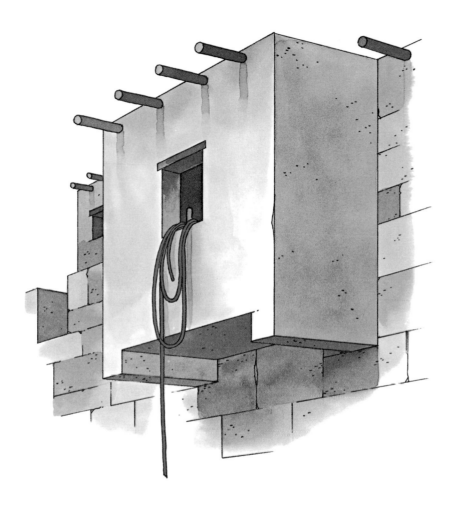

What Is in Your Window?
My Favorite Thing: Rahab's Scarlet Cord

Rahab's house is different from the one where you live. It was built on a city wall. Do you see it? Rahab must have loved her home as you love yours. But one day two men came to her house. They were spies. Somehow Rahab knew that their people, the Israelites, would capture her city. What would happen to her then? "I will help you if you help me," Rahab told these men. Then Rahab helped these men escape. She let them down the wall with this scarlet cord. "Keep this cord in your window," the men told her. "No one will hurt you as long as it is there." Of course Rahab kept it there.

WHAT DO YOU SEE?
Where is Rahab's house? What do you think it was like to live here? Where is the scarlet cord? Where are the walls?

A TIME TO SHARE
1. *Who did Rahab help? How?*
2. *How did these men help her?*
3. *When was Rahab safe?*
4. *Do you do what you know is best? Why?*

May I Have Some of That?
My Favorite Thing: Lemonade

When was the last time you were hot and tired? Were you thirsty? Were you ready for a cold glass of something to drink? This boy has been doing something that made him hot and tired. What do you think he was doing? Mother knows he is thirsty. That's why she has made a pitcher of cold lemonade. Mothers know when boys and girls get thirsty. Aren't you glad they do?

WHAT DO YOU SEE?
Point to some things that tell you this is lemonade in the pitcher. Where is the lemon? What is next to it? Where is the sugar? Where does the water come from?

A TIME TO SHARE
1. *What is Mother holding in her hands?*
2. *What do you do that makes you thirsty?*
3. *Do you remember to say "thank you" when Mother makes lemonade for you?*

Lots of Pockets

My Favorite Thing: My Pockets

What would we do without pockets? This boy likes his pockets. He puts all kinds of things in them. But boys aren't the only people who like pockets. Mothers like them too. And Fathers always use their pockets. Sometimes girls put handkerchiefs and other things in their pockets. Don't you think a pocket is one of your favorite things? What would you do without pockets?

A TIME TO SHARE

1. Do you like pockets?

2. Can you name each type of clothing that has a pocket?

3. What do you put into your pockets?

WHAT DO YOU SEE?

How many pockets can you count? Point to each one. What do you think each person can put into each pocket?

Look at What We're Eating

My Favorite Thing: Goldfish

Do you see what I see? It's like a little ocean or lake with glass walls. This girl likes her aquarium. She likes to feed the goldfish in it. They are pretty, don't you think? But look! She is giving the goldfish something small. It doesn't look at all like the food her sister is giving Kitty. Do you suppose Kitty would like the goldfish food? Would the goldfish like Kitty's food? You wouldn't want to eat either kind of food, would you? That's the way God planned it. It's a good idea to do things the way God planned them, isn't it?

A TIME TO SHARE

1. *What are some foods that you eat?*
2. *Why would you not like Kitty's food?*
3. *Do you thank God for your food?*
4. *Will you do that now?*

WHAT DO YOU SEE?
Where is Kitty? Why doesn't Kitty swim in the aquarium? Why don't the goldfish walk around on the floor?

Run, Puppy, Run!

My Favorite Thing: My Puppy

Run, Puppy, run! Catch the ball! Puppy is running, isn't he? The boy rolls the ball. Puppy chases it. The girl claps her hands. Puppy jumps and barks. Do you like to play with your puppy like this? Puppy likes to do what the boy and girl tell him to do. When the boy tells him to chase the ball, he loves to chase it. When the girl claps her hands and tells the puppy to jump, he loves to jump. That's because Puppy knows he should obey. Do you like to do what Mother or Father says? Do you like to do what Jesus wants you to do?

A TIME TO SHARE

1. *What is the puppy doing?*
2. *Who told him to do this?*
3. *Why does he like to obey?*
4. *Why do you like to obey?*

WHAT DO YOU SEE?
Whose room is this? How do you know? Point to some things that tell you this is a boy's room.

Blow That Trumpet!

My Favorite Thing: Gideon's Trumpet

Do you play a trumpet? If you do, it certainly isn't like this one. Gideon did not play his trumpet in an orchestra. He did not take music lessons. He did not play it in a school program. When Gideon blew on his trumpet, his soldiers began to shout. That's what God told them to do. It was God's way to help them win a battle. Wouldn't you like to hear Gideon blow on his trumpet?

WHAT DO YOU SEE?
Where is Gideon's trumpet? It is made from an animal horn. Do you think Gideon is blowing on it now?

A TIME TO SHARE
1. *What happened when Gideon blew on his trumpet?*
2. *Who told him to do this?*
3. *Why should we do what God says?*

There He Is!

My Favorite Thing: A Frog

There he is! Do you see him? The boy sees that big frog sitting on a stone. The girl sees him too. Do you think the frog sees them? You can tell that he does. He is looking at them. But what is that frog doing? Is he hopping around? Is he sitting there, looking at the boy and girl? Would you like to be a frog? Why not? Do you think that frog would like to be a boy or girl? Why not? Aren't you glad God made you to be you? Aren't you glad He made the frog to be a frog?

WHAT DO YOU SEE?
Where is this? Point to four things that tell you this is a pond. Why would you not see these four things in your living room?

A TIME TO SHARE
1. *What is on the stone?*
2. *How is he different from you? What can you do that he can't?*
3. *Why are you glad you are you?*

Good Morning, Merry Sunshine

My Favorite Thing: Sunshine

Good morning, merry sunshine! It's time to get up. This boy is thinking of all the fun things he will do today. He wants to go outside to play. Do you think he is glad to see the sunshine this morning? The sunshine feels warm and friendly on his face. How would he feel if it were raining? Would that feel warm and friendly? How would he feel if he were sick and could not go out when the sun is shining? Would he feel sad or happy then? Are you glad for sunshine? This boy is.

WHAT DO YOU SEE?
How do you know that this is morning? Why do you think it is not evening? Why do you think it is not night? Why do you think it is not noon?

A TIME TO SHARE
1. *What does the boy see outside?*
2. *Why is he happy?*
3. *What do you do when the sun is shining? What do you do when it isn't?*

A Special Time with Father

My Favorite Thing: Butterflies

Oh, what a wonderful day for a walk! What a wonderful day to sit in the grass and talk! You can see that's what Father and his boy are doing. You can see some special things that they see too. The boy is pointing to some beautiful things flying around the flowers. What are they? What do you think he is saying about them? Do you like to go for a walk with Father or Mother? Do you like to talk with them about special things, like butterflies? Why do you think God is pleased when you do things like that?

A TIME TO SHARE

1. *What are Father and the boy doing?*
2. *What do you think they are saying?*
3. *What would you say if you were here?*

WHAT DO YOU SEE?
Point to some things you would not see on a city street. Can you name each one? Why do you think this is not winter? Why do you think it is not night?

Something Cool

My Favorite Thing: Ice Cubes

You wouldn't want ice cubes when you are building a snowman, would you? And who wants an iced drink when you're sledding? But you can see that these boys and girls aren't doing either of those things. On a hot summer day, ice cubes are just the thing. Think of the wonderful things you can do with ice cubes when you're hot and thirsty. What are these boys and girls doing with them?

A TIME TO SHARE

1. Why do you like ice cubes when you are hot and thirsty? What do they do?

2. What do you like to drink when you're cold? Why?

WHAT DO YOU SEE?
How do you know this is a summer day? How do you know it is not winter? Point to the ice cubes. Where is the drink? What will they put it in?

The Brave Hunter

My Favorite Thing: Arrow

"I want to be a brave hunter," says the boy. Father knows the boy wants to do this. But he knows the boy is not ready yet. He must learn how to shoot an arrow from a bow. He must learn how to hit a target. He must do it again and again until he does not miss. "Someday you may be a brave hunter," Father tells his boy. "Today we must learn to shoot an arrow from the bow." The boy is glad Father is helping him. He is glad Father will teach him how to do this. Aren't you glad fathers and mothers teach us things?

A TIME TO SHARE

1. What is Father helping the boy do?

2. Why is the boy glad for Father?

3. What do you like Father or Mother to do with you?

WHAT DO YOU SEE?
What is that on the tree? What is the boy holding? What is Father holding? Where will the arrow go when the boy does his best?

I Found a Feather

My Favorite Thing: A Feather

Look what this girl found! The geese do not mind. They did not need this feather. So it fell from one of them. But the girl thinks it is special to find the feather. She wants Father to see it. She will take it home to show some others. Who do you think will see it? The feather will remind her of the fun Father and she had feeding the geese. It will remind her that it is a special time when she can be with Father. Don't you think so too?

WHAT DO YOU SEE?
Where did this feather come from? Point to the geese. What do you think that bag is near Father? What will Father and the girl do with the feed?

A TIME TO SHARE
1. *What did the girl find?*
2. *Why do geese have feathers?*
3. *Who gave them their feathers?*

94

Watch Out, Lion!

My Favorite Thing: David's Sling

That lion better watch out! If he tries to kill David's sheep, he is in trouble. You can see what is about to happen. Do you know what David will do? He will whirl that rock around and around. It will go so fast that you can hardly see it. Then he will let it go toward the lion. That lion better watch out! David is very good with that sling.

WHAT DO YOU SEE?
Where is the lion? What do you think he is trying to do? Where is the rock in David's sling? What will David do with it?

A TIME TO SHARE
1. *What does David do with his sling?*
2. *How does this protect his sheep?*
3. *Do you think David's sheep felt safe with him? Why?*

95

A Day on Dandelion Hill
My Favorite Thing: Dandelions

Oh, for a day on Dandelion Hill! That's what this family calls their favorite picnic spot. Can you think why they call it that? "Look at me!" says the girl. You can see what she is doing with a dandelion. "Look at me too!" says the boy. He is having fun with a dandelion too, isn't he? Even Father is doing something with a dandelion. No wonder the family calls this "Dandelion Hill." Would you like to go with them for a day on Dandelion Hill?

WHAT DO YOU SEE?
What color are dandelions when you can blow them to the wind? What color are they when you can't do this?

A TIME TO SHARE
1. *What is this family doing?*
2. *What are they doing with dandelions?*
3. *Is this summer or winter? Is it day or night? How do you know?*

96

Around and Around I Go!

My Favorite Thing: Merry-go-round

Around and around I go. But where am I going? I am going to see Mother and Father. Do you see them smiling and waving to me? Then off I go around the world. I am going to exciting places far away. Around and around I go. Up and down I go. Then I come back to Mother and Father again. They are always glad to see me come back. And I am always glad to see them too.

A TIME TO SHARE

1. *What is the girl riding on?*
2. *Where is she going?*
3. *Why are Mother and Father smiling?*
4. *Why is the girl smiling?*

WHAT DO YOU SEE?
Do you see the girl's little brother? Why isn't he riding on the merry-go-round? What is Father holding in his hand? Do you suppose Mother and little brother will share that?

What Are You Doing Up There?

My Favorite Thing: A Woodpecker

Listen! Do you hear what I hear? Do you hear that noise up in the tree? Do you know what is making that noise? These girls and the boy have found it. They see this bird pecking on the tree. Do you see it? Why do you think the woodpecker is doing that? It's fun to watch a woodpecker peck. A robin doesn't do that. A chickadee doesn't do that. But God made this woodpecker so that he would peck on a tree. God makes some interesting things, doesn't He?

A TIME TO SHARE

1. What is the woodpecker doing?

2. Why does he do things this way?

3. What would you like to say to the woodpecker?

WHAT DO YOU SEE?
Point to the woodpecker. What part of him hits the tree? What does he use to hold onto the tree? What does he use to fly?

What Would We Do without Grass?

My Favorite Thing: Grass

What a wonderful day to be outside! Do you see what those boys are doing? They are rolling down the hill. But it would be no fun if that hill were muddy, would it? That's why the boys are glad for the grass. You know how much fun it is to roll in the grass, don't you? Do you ever do that? Father likes grass too. He likes to mow the grass and make the lawn look neat. Something else in this picture likes grass. Do you know what it is? Why do you think the cow likes the grass? What does the cow do with it?

A TIME TO SHARE

1. *What are the boys doing with grass?*
2. *What is Father doing with it?*
3. *What is the cow doing with it?*
4. *Why are you glad for grass?*

WHAT DO YOU SEE?

Where do you see more grass, in town or in the country? Where is this? Point to some places where you see grass.

Something to Eat

My Favorite Thing: Elijah's Ravens

This man Elijah has nothing to eat. But no one else in the land has much to eat either. That's because it has not rained for a long time. How can crops grow without rain? How can people have food if the crops don't grow? But look! Do you see those birds? They are bringing some food to Elijah. God sent them. He wants Elijah to have something to eat. He is a wonderful God, isn't He?

A TIME TO SHARE

1. *What are those birds doing?*
2. *Why does Elijah need them?*
3. *Who sent the ravens?*
4. *What should Elijah say to God? Why?*

WHAT DO YOU SEE?
What are the birds bringing to Elijah? Why? How many ravens do you see? Point to the food. Point to Elijah.

100

Come Up to My House

My Favorite Thing: My Tree House

Look at those boys! Where are they? Are they in the kitchen? Are they in the grocery store? Of course not. If you've ever had a tree house, you know where they arc. And you know they are having fun, because tree houses are fun. But they are having more fun because they are playing togethcr. What are some special things you like to do with your friends? Where are some spccial places you like to play with them?

A TIME TO SHARE

1. *Who are some of your best friends?*
2. *What do you like to do with them?*
3. *Why do you like to play with them?*
4. *Who likes to see you have fun?*

WHAT DO YOU SEE?

How do you know this is a tree house? How do the boys get up to it? Why do they have to be careful when they are playing up here?

Four Friends and a Fountain

My Favorite Thing: A Fountain

Now this looks like fun on a hot summer day. Who doesn't like cool running water at a time like this? Do you? These boys do. They have been running and playing in the park. They are hot and tired. Now see what they are doing. Nobody thinks this is wrong. You can see the man is smiling. He is glad the boys can enjoy the fountain. Do you think he would like to do this too? Don't you think these boys are good friends? How can you tell?

WHAT DO YOU SEE?
Why do you think this is in town? Why isn't it on a farm? What do you see that tells you that? Why do you think this is summer? Why isn't it winter?

A TIME TO SHARE
1. *What are the boys doing?*
2. *Why are they doing this?*
3. *Do you do fun things with your friends?*
4. *Are you glad for friends?*

Time to Eat

My Favorite Thing: An Elephant

Now there's an animal you would not want for a pet. But it is fun to go to visit this fellow. The boy and girl like to watch this elephant eat. Mother and Father like to watch him too. Do you see how the elephant picks up his food? Do you see the man who feeds the elephant? Aren't you glad you don't eat what the elephant eats? But the elephant would not want to eat your breakfast either. That's the way God made the elephant. And that's the way God made you.

A TIME TO SHARE

1. What is the elephant eating?

2. What did you eat for breakfast?

3. Would you want to be an elephant? Why not? Aren't you glad you're you?

WHAT DO YOU SEE?

Where are these people? How do you know they are not in their own backyard? Is the elephant bigger or smaller than the boy and girl?

My Mother Is a Pretty Mother

My Favorite Thing: My Mother's Smile

Do you like to look at Mother's face? This girl does. Sometimes Mother is sad. Sometimes she is happy. And sometimes she tells me "Don't do that," or "Shhhhh, you must be quiet." Mother's face changes many times each day. This girl likes it best when Mother smiles. Mother's eyes twinkle and her lips look soft and warm. It reminds the girl of sunshine on a beautiful summer day. Do you like to look at Mother's face? Do you like to see Mother smile? How do you feel when she does?

WHAT DO YOU SEE?
Point to the nose on Mother's face. Point to her eyes. Can you find her lips? When Mother smiles, how do each of these change?

A TIME TO SHARE
1. *Who is with this girl?*
2. *Do you think she is happy or sad? Why?*
3. *What do you think the girl is thinking?*

Big Stones for a Wall
My Favorite Thing: Nehemiah's Wall

Look! Do you see all those big stones? How would you like to move those around? How would you like to build a wall with them? Nehemiah did. Of course he had some help. You can see all those men working. They are building this wall to keep enemies out. People had to do that in Nehemiah's time. If they didn't, they would get hurt. That's why everyone worked together. Each person had to do something. That's a good way to do it, isn't it?

WHAT DO YOU SEE?
How many men do you see? What is each one doing? What does that man on top of the wall have? What do you think he is doing?

A TIME TO SHARE
1. *What are Nehemiah and his friends doing? Why is this important?*
2. *Why are they helping each other?*
3. *How can you help others in your family?*

105

I Smell Something Good

My Favorite Thing: Pancakes

It didn't take long for this boy to get dressed. He smelled something wonderful as soon as he woke up. Have you ever done that? You can see what is making that wonderful smell. Mother dips up some pancake batter with her big spoon. *Plop!* She puts the batter on the griddle. Before long the boy will turn over the pancake. It will be toasty brown on the other side. Ummm. Can't you taste that wonderful pancake? What would you put on it?

WHAT DO YOU SEE?
Point to each thing Mother and the boy used to make the pancakes. Can you name each one?

A TIME TO SHARE

1. *What is Mother making?*
2. *Why is it fun to help Mother?*
3. *What do you like to do with Mother?*

Do You Want a Clothespin?

My Favorite Thing: Mother's Clothespins

"Oh, how I love to help Mother hang up the clothes." That's what this girl says. Of course she can't reach up to the clothesline, can she? But Mother can. And the girl can reach up to Mother. Here she comes with the bag of clothespins. She will hand them up to Mother, one at a time. Don't you think Mother is glad to have a helper today? And don't you think the girl is having fun with Mother's clothespins?

A TIME TO SHARE

1. Why is the girl so happy?

2. Why is Mother happy?

3. Why is it fun to be a helper?

4. How can you help your mother?

WHAT DO YOU SEE?

What is Mother hanging on the line? Do you see some clothes that she will soon hang up? Point to them. What is holding the clothes on the line? Point to them.

Up in My Swing

My Favorite Thing: My Swing

Oh, I love to go on my swing. Father pushes and up I go. Then back again to Father. It's something like flying, except without wings. Up and back. Up and back. But swinging would not be as much fun without Father or Mother to help me. That makes it special. Do you like to go up in your swing? Do you like to feel the wind go past your face when you swing?

WHAT DO YOU SEE?
What holds the swing up? Do you think those ropes are strong? Do you suppose Father checked to make sure they would not break?

A TIME TO SHARE
1. *Why is this girl having fun?*
2. *Why is it more fun with Father there?*
3. *What do you like to do with Father or Mother?*

Whoooooo

My Favorite Thing: My Tent

This boy is a brave boy, isn't he? He has gone camping, all alone. Of course, he is doing it in his own backyard. And he does have Puppy with him to keep him company. You can see that he has his flashlight and sleeping bag too. He is sure with all those things that he will be a brave boy. Oh, oh! Do you hear what I hear? There's a wild animal. It goes *WHOOOOOO*. Now the boy is not so brave. He is afraid. What if that wild animal hurts him? Then he hears something else. There is Father, "just checking" to see if the boy is all right. Now the boy feels brave again. When Father is with him, everything seems good again.

A TIME TO SHARE

1. *Why was the boy afraid?*
2. *How did he feel when Father came?*
3. *When you are afraid, who do you want with you? Who is with you at all times?*

WHAT DO YOU SEE?

Point to some things that tell you the boy is camping. Point to the animal that went *WHOOOOOO*. What is it?

What Is That?

My Favorite Thing: A Scroll

This man is reading a book. It doesn't look much like your favorite book, does it? But this was the way people made books in Bible times. A book like this was called a scroll. A person had to write each word on this scroll. There was no other way to do it. They did not have printing presses. So it was hard work to make one book. That's why there were only a few books. That's why people wrote only important things like God's Word. This man is glad. Someone put God's Word on this scroll. He is glad to read it to others.

A TIME TO SHARE

1. *What is this man reading?*
2. *Why is he glad to read it?*
3. *Why are you glad to read God's Word?*

WHAT DO YOU SEE?
Point to the two ends of the scroll. Do you see how the paper rolls up on each end? How many hands does this man need to hold the scroll? Why?

A Special Book

My Favorite Thing: My Bible

This boy has found something good to read. It is not a comic book. It is not even a storybook. Do you know what he is reading? Mother and Father gave this Bible to the boy. They know it will tell the boy about God. That makes the Bible a special book, doesn't it? Is that why you like to read your Bible too?

A TIME TO SHARE

1. *What is the boy doing?*
2. *What does the Bible tell him?*
3. *Why do you like to read your Bible?*
4. *What will your Bible do for you?*

WHAT DO YOU SEE?
How do you know this is a boy's room? Point to some things that tell you that it is. Why do you think the boy likes to read his Bible?

Even the Kitchen Sink Is Fun

My Favorite Thing: Our Kitchen Sink

I see a family working together. Do you? Mother is bringing the dirty dishes from the table. Father is taking out the garbage. And this boy and girl are being good helpers, aren't they? Would you think the kitchen sink could be fun? This boy and girl think it is fun because they like to help Mother and Father. They laugh and talk about fun things while they wash the dishes and dry them. Do you like to be a family helper? It's fun, isn't it?

WHAT DO YOU SEE?
What has this family just done? How do you know? Can you point to some of the different kinds of dishes?

A TIME TO SHARE
1. *Do the boy and girl look happy?*
2. *Why do you think they are happy?*
3. *Why wouldn't this family look happy if Mother was doing all the work?*

Come into My Castle
My Favorite Thing: A Big Box

"Will you come into my castle?" asks the boy. It's really nothing but a big box, isn't it? But it could be a castle. Or it could be a train going somewhere. Or you could pretend that it's a tree house on a big cloud in the sky. This boy and girl have thought of at least a dozen things their box can be for them. You may think of a dozen more. Whatever you think a big box is, it's one of our favorite things.

WHAT DO YOU SEE?
What do the boy and girl have? Who is playing there with them? Think of five things that could have been in this box when it came to them.

A TIME TO SHARE
1. *Why is a big box so much fun?*
2. *Pretend you are playing in this big box. What five things could it be?*

A Parade Goes By

My Favorite Thing: A Parade

How can you stand still when a parade goes by? This boy and girl can't. They want to jump up and down. Or perhaps they would even march in the parade if they could. Do you know why? Can you hear the drum go *boom, boom, boom*? Can you hear that tuba go *oom pa pa, oom pa pa*? And how do you think that other horn goes? Even Father is ready to do something. No wonder a parade is a favorite thing. We can't stand still when a parade goes by.

WHAT DO YOU SEE?
How many people do you see in the parade? What is each person playing? How does each instrument sound?

A TIME TO SHARE
1. *Why are Father and the boy and girl so excited? Would you be excited?*
2. *What would you say if you were here?*
3. *What would you do?*

A Way to Catch Fish

My Favorite Thing: Fishermen's Nets

This man has been working. He still is! He did not put on a suit and tie. He did not go to an office. He did not drive a fire engine or fly a plane. This man put these nets into a lake. Then he pulled them in again with fish in them. That's because he is a fisherman. When he stopped fishing, he hung his nets up to dry. Do you see the big one? The man is fixing the little one. It must have torn on some rocks. Would you like to go fishing this way? Do you wish the man would show you how?

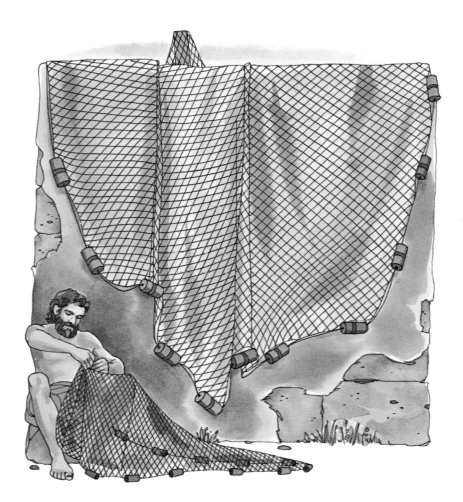

A TIME TO SHARE

1. *What is this man doing to the nets?*
2. *How does he use the nets to fish?*
3. *What would you like to ask the man?*
4. *Do you think Jesus saw a man like this?*

WHAT DO YOU SEE?
Which net is drying? Which one is the man fixing? Do you see the little floats along the edge of the nets? They help that part of the net to stay on top of the water.

115

Hello Up There

My Favorite Thing: A Giraffe

Why is everyone looking up? You won't see the giraffe if you look down, will you? Of course we all want to see the giraffe. This family does. And so do you. A giraffe is one of our favorite things, isn't it? Where else would you see a neck that long? Where else would you see such a funny face? We wouldn't want the giraffe for a pet, but he is fun to visit at the zoo.

A TIME TO SHARE

1. *Why do you like the giraffe?*
2. *Why would it not be a good pet?*
3. *How are you different from the giraffe?*
4. *Why would you rather be you?*

WHAT DO YOU SEE?
Why do you think this is a zoo? Point to some things that you would not see at your school.

Castles in the Sand

My Favorite Thing: Sand Castles

These people are having fun. They like to do things together. You can see that they do. Today they are having fun together at the beach. But they are not swimming. They are not walking along the sand. They are doing something you may want to do. While Mother fixes lunch, Father builds a castle. It is not like a real castle where a king lives. This castle is made of sand. It is called a sand castle. Do you think the boy and girl are having fun? Would you have fun doing this?

A TIME TO SHARE

1. *What is Mother doing? What is Father doing with the boy and girl?*
2. *Why are they having fun?*
3. *What do you do with your family?*

WHAT DO YOU SEE?

What do you see that tells you this is the beach? What do you see that you would not find in your living room? How many birds can you find?

A Cup of Water

My Favorite Thing: Grandfather's Pump

Where do you get your water? Do you get it from a pump like this? What do you do to get it? This girl is having fun at Grandfather's house. She does many things differently here than at home. The girl does not have a pump like this at home. She likes to get a drink of water at this pump. Grandfather pumps the handle up and down. That makes the water come out into the cup. Of course some of it doesn't go in the cup. You can see it, can't you? Puppy sees this extra water. He wants a drink too. Do you like a drink of cold water?

WHAT DO YOU SEE?
Who is getting a drink of water? Do you see two others who are drinking? What is Grandfather doing? How do you know this is not in the city?

A TIME TO SHARE
1. *Where does water come from?*
2. *Who gives us water to drink?*
3. *Do you thank God for water?*
4. *Will you do that now?*

Blowing Bubbles
My Favorite Thing: Bubbles

It's a summer day. That's a good time to blow bubbles, isn't it? These boys and girls think so. They have come to this backyard to do it. Look at all those bubbles. Are there more bubbles than boys and girls? Can you count the bubbles? Can you count the boys and girls? What do you think these boys and girls are saying? Why do you think they are having fun together?

WHAT DO YOU SEE?
Do you think this is a windy day? Why not? What is the puppy doing? Who has the biggest bubble? Which is the smallest bubble?

A TIME TO SHARE
1. *Why is blowing bubbles so much fun?*
2. *Why is it more fun to do this with your friends?*
3. *What colors do you see in a bubble?*

Look at This!

My Favorite Thing: Grandfather's Lantern

Have you seen a lantern like that? It's something you probably don't have at your house. But this boy's grandfather has it. He puts oil in the bottom of the lantern. Then he lights the top with a match. Grandfather likes to take his lantern to the barn. He likes to show the boy some of the special things out there. Now here is a very special thing today. Grandfather wants to show the boy the new colt. That's something worth seeing, isn't it? And it's even better to see the new colt in the light from Grandfather's lantern.

WHAT DO YOU SEE?
Why do you think this is a barn? Point to some things you would not see in your living room. Point to Grandfather's lantern. How is your lantern different?

A TIME TO SHARE
1. *What is Grandfather showing the boy?*
2. *Could they see without the lantern?*
3. *Think of the different kinds of lights in your house. Are you glad for each one?*

120

Sowing Seed

My Favorite Thing: The Sower's Seed

This man is throwing seed on the ground. That's the way people planted their crops in Bible times. Of course people don't do that today. They use tractors and planters. Wouldn't this man be surprised to see those things? But seeds grow no matter how we plant them. These seeds will grow up into plants. Then the man will get the new grain from them. This is the way the man and his family will get food to eat.

A TIME TO SHARE

1. Why is the man sowing this seed?

2. How will he get food from it?

3. Who sends the sunshine and rain?

4. Who gives us our food? Let's thank Him!

WHAT DO YOU SEE?

Do you see the seed? Where is the man getting this seed? Point to the pouch where he carries it. Point to the ground where the seed will grow.

Here It Comes!

My Favorite Thing: A Fire Engine

Here it comes! It's making a terrible noise. Do you hear the siren whining? Do you see the red lights flashing? Do you hear that big motor roar as the fire engine races past? These boys see and hear these things. They think the fire engine is exciting. One boy wants to run after it. Do you think he will catch it? Why not? The boys are glad for the fire engine. They are glad for the firemen. If their house catches fire, these firemen will come in a hurry. Aren't you glad for firemen too?

A TIME TO SHARE

1. *What do firemen do for you?*
2. *Why are you glad for them?*
3. *What do you like about a fire engine?*

WHAT DO YOU SEE?

Do you see the smoke? Do you suppose that is where the firemen are going? How many firemen do you see? Do you think there is another? Why?

Here We Are on a Sunny Day

My Favorite Thing: My Sunglasses

Here we are on a bright, sunny day. Father is watering the lawn. The sun makes the lawn thirsty. It needs a drink of water just as you do. This boy and girl have come out to watch. They like to come into the backyard on a sunny day. But today the boy has something special. The girl thinks he is funny with those big sunglasses. Do you think so too? But the boy likes to wear them anyway. He can see better when he does. Do you know why?

A TIME TO SHARE

1. *How do you know this is summer?*
2. *What would you not see in winter?*
3. *Why is the boy wearing sunglasses?*
4. *What do you like about sunshine?*

WHAT DO YOU SEE?
Why do you think this is the family's backyard? Point to some things that tell you it is not their living room.

Let's Go to the Pond

My Favorite Thing: Cattails

Do you like to visit a pond? There are all kinds of interesting things there. Some ponds have frogs. They make strange noises, don't they? Some ponds have ducks or geese. And some ponds have cattails growing along the edge. Do you see them here? Do you think they look like a cat's tail?

WHAT DO YOU SEE?

How do you know this is a pond? Why do you think it is not a street downtown? What do you see here that you do not see there?

A TIME TO SHARE

1. *Where are Father and the boy?*
2. *Why do you think they are having fun?*
3. *Why is it fun to do special things together with Father or Mother?*

Time for a Picnic

My Favorite Thing: Our Picnic Table

Look at all that food. Do you suppose this is a picnic? I see hot dogs and buns, pickles and catsup, and a box of potato chips. Oh, yes, there is also something good to drink on a summer day. Isn't it fun to have a backyard picnic with friends? But how could you have a picnic without your picnic table? That's one of my favorite things. Is it yours?

A TIME TO SHARE

1. *What are these boys and girls doing?*
2. *Why do you think they are having fun?*
3. *How do you have fun with friends?*
4. *Why is this better than fighting?*

WHAT DO YOU SEE?

How many picnic things can you find? Point to the hot dogs and buns. Find the jar of pickles and the bottle of catsup. What else do you see?

Listen! What Do You Hear?

My Favorite Thing: My Ears

Listen to that beautiful music! Listen to the birds singing! Listen to Mother reading that wonderful story to you! Listen! Listen! Listen! When you listen carefully all day, what do you hear? This boy is listening to his favorite music. That's something he likes to do. He hears his puppy breathing and making puppy noises. Do you think this boy is glad he can listen? Do you think he is glad for his ears? Who should he thank for giving them to him?

A TIME TO SHARE

1. *Does the boy hear with his eyes, ears, nose, or mouth?*

2. *What does he do with those other things? Who should he thank for them?*

WHAT DO YOU SEE?
Where is the music coming from? What room do you think this boy is in? Is it the kitchen? Why not? Is it the boy's room? Why do you think so?

126

Who Was in That Tree?

My Favorite Thing: The Tree Zaccheus Climbed

This tree looks like any other tree. But it isn't. This one is special. It helped a man see Jesus. Do you remember how? Zaccheus remembers. He heard that Jesus was in town. He wanted to see Jesus. But Zaccheus was a little man. And there were people crowding around Jesus. Zaccheus couldn't even see Jesus. What could he do? Then Zaccheus had a good idea. He climbed this tree. Then he saw Jesus. Jesus saw Zaccheus too. He even went to Zaccheus' house for dinner. That's how Zaccheus became Jesus' friend. It's a good thing that tree was there, isn't it?

A TIME TO SHARE

1. Why did Zaccheus climb this tree?

2. Who did he see? What happened then?

3. Why are you glad when someone becomes Jesus' friend?

WHAT DO YOU SEE?
Point to the tree. Where do you think Zaccheus was when he saw Jesus? Where do you think he lived?

Stay Over There
My Favorite Thing: A Strong Fence

Oh, oh! Do you see what I see? This boy and his father do. That big bull looks mean. What if he starts to chase Father and the boy? He could hurt them, couldn't he? But look at that strong fence. Someone put that there to keep the bull in his pasture. Father and the boy are glad for the strong fence. Don't you think they should be?

WHAT DO YOU SEE?
What do you see that tells you this is not in a city? What do you see that tells you what Father and the boy are doing?

A TIME TO SHARE
1. *Why are Father and the boy concerned?*
2. *What could the bull do?*
3. *But why can't the bull get to them?*
4. *Are you glad for some fences? Which ones?*

Something Good

My Favorite Thing: Popcorn

You can always smell popcorn before you see it. This family smelled that wonderful buttered popcorn smell. Of course, when you smell it, you want it. "Please, oh please, oh please," the boy and girl said. They really didn't have to say that. Father and Mother wanted some buttered popcorn too. When they saw the cart and the popcorn man, they knew they had found what they wanted. Would you like to be here with them?

WHAT DO YOU SEE?
Who do you think will pay for this popcorn? Why do you think so? But who will eat the popcorn? Who made it? Could Mother have paid? How do you know?

A TIME TO SHARE
1. *What are these people buying?*
2. *Are you glad you can smell and taste good things? Will you thank God that you can?*

Something to Love
My Favorite Thing: My Pet

Do you have a puppy? This boy does. He likes to play with his puppy. He likes to feed it and take care of it. That's what we should do for our puppies, shouldn't we? But someone takes care of the boy. Do you see who that person is? She is smiling at the boy. Someone else takes care of the boy too. He is at work. Who is that? And there is one other Person who takes care of the boy. He watches the boy all the time. He is the boy's best Friend. Who is He?

WHAT DO YOU SEE?
How many smiles do you see? Why is the boy smiling? Why is Mother smiling? The puppy isn't smiling. How does he show that he is happy?

A TIME TO SHARE
1. *Who takes care of the puppy?*
2. *Who takes care of the boy?*
3. *How does Mother take care of him?*
4. *How does God take care of him?*

Squeeze This Next Please

My Favorite Thing: Oranges

Why do you think oranges are called oranges? Why not call them greens or pinks or blues? This girl and her mother like oranges. Sometimes they like to eat them. Sometimes they like to squeeze the juice from them. Which are they doing here?

A TIME TO SHARE

1. What are Mother and the girl doing?

2. What do you like about oranges?

3. Are oranges a fruit, grain, or nut?

4. Are you glad God gives us oranges?

WHAT DO YOU SEE?

How many glasses do you see? Who do you think will drink those other two glasses? What has Mother used to get this orange juice? Name each item.

Someone We Love

My Favorite Thing: Our Telephone

Listen! Do you hear something ringing? What is it? This girl heard it ringing. She was the first person to get to the phone. You can tell by the smile on her face that someone special is calling. Who do you think that is? Could it be the people in the picture?

WHAT DO YOU SEE?

Whose picture do you see? Is the girl smiling or frowning? This will tell you that someone she loves is calling.

A TIME TO SHARE

1. *How do you know that the girl and her family love Grandfather and Grandmother?*
2. *Why should we tell our family that we love them?*

Two Little Coins

My Favorite Thing: The Widow's Coins

How many coins do you have? Would you like to count them? This poor woman had only two coins. They were not worth much. Each coin, called a mite, was worth less than a penny. But that was all the money she had. What do you think this woman is doing with her two coins? You can see that she is giving them away. She is in God's house. This strange thing is like the offering plate at your church. People put their offerings for God there. Now you know what she is doing. Now you know she is giving all she has to God.

A TIME TO SHARE

1. *What is this woman doing?*
2. *How much is she giving to God?*
3. *How much is she keeping?*
4. *Why should we give money to God?*

WHAT DO YOU SEE?
Where is the widow's coin? Do you think the other coin is in the offering box? Point to the offering box. How is it different from what you use in Sunday School?

Is That for Me?

My Favorite Thing: Our Toaster

Ummmm. You can almost smell that toast, can't you? Mother is putting butter on the hot toast. Next she will put on some jam. Do you see the butter? Do you see the jam? The boy sees them. He smells them too. That's why he came running into the kitchen. You would run to the kitchen too if Mother had some hot toast for you, wouldn't you?

A TIME TO SHARE

1. *How many pieces of toast do you see?*
2. *Who are they for?*
3. *If you had an extra piece of toast, who would you share it with?*

WHAT DO YOU SEE?
Where is the toaster? How do you know that's what it is? What does the toaster do? What did it do for this mother and her boy?

Look What I Found

My Favorite Thing: Colored Leaves

It's that time of year again. Do you see the colored leaves? How many colors can you find? This boy and girl are looking for some leaves of each color. You can see that they are having fun. "Look what I found!" the boy says. "And look what I found!" the girl says. Puppy has found something too. Do you see what it is? It's fun to find new things, isn't it? What new thing have you found this week?

A TIME TO SHARE

1. What are the boy and girl doing?

2. What are some fun things you like to do?

3. Why does Jesus like us to have fun?

WHAT DO YOU SEE?

What time of year is this? Is it winter? How do you know? Is it spring? What would you see then? Is it summer? How would the trees look then?

Guess What We Will Make
My Favorite Thing: My Apron

Look at that pretty apron the girl is wearing. It is almost like Mother's apron. Do you know why they are wearing aprons? They are getting ready to make something. Mother brought the milk and eggs from the refrigerator. Do you see them? The girl took the pancake mix from the cupboard. And look at all those other things they will use to make the pancakes. Can you name each one?

WHAT DO YOU SEE?
Mother and the girl have nine things which will help them make pancakes. Point to each one and tell what it is.

A TIME TO SHARE
1. *Why do you think Mother and the girl are both smiling?*
2. *Do you like to do things together?*
3. *Why is that fun?*

The Biggest Smile

My Favorite Thing: A Jack-o'-lantern

I see four faces here, don't you? One big face is smiling. That's why everyone else is smiling at the jack-o'-lantern. Of course, he could be doing some other things with his face. How would his face look if he were frowning? How would it look if he were puzzled? And how would it look if he were angry? This jack-o'-lantern is fun to have around. Don't you think it's always more fun to have a smiling face than a frowning face?

A TIME TO SHARE

1. Why are the boy and girl smiling?

2. Why do you like to smile?

3. Why would a smiling face please Jesus more than a frowning face?

WHAT DO YOU SEE?

What month do you think this is? Why do you think so? What is the jack-o'-lantern made of? How did he get his face?

137

Ummm

My Favorite Thing: Homemade Bread

Do you smell it baking in the oven? What smells better than Mother's homemade bread? Ummm. And what tastes better too? You have tried some, haven't you? Do you remember how the butter melted on the warm bread? And wasn't the jam or jelly good on that buttered bread? Ummm. Would you like to eat some now? This boy and girl would.

WHAT DO YOU SEE?
Point to each thing Mother has used to make the homemade bread. Can you name each one? Point to the bread, the butter, the jam, and the knife.

A TIME TO SHARE
1. *What is Mother doing now?*
2. *What are the boy and girl doing?*
3. *What should they say to Mother?*
4. *Do you thank God for good food?*

Bread and Fish

My Favorite Thing: A Boy's Lunch

You've probably never seen a lunch like that before. You wouldn't take it to school in your lunch box, would you? But this boy thought it was quite a fine lunch. He came here to listen to Jesus. So did 5,000 other people. But no one else thought to bring lunch. No one brought lunch except this boy. How could one boy's lunch feed 5,000 people? Usually it couldn't. But Jesus was there. He broke pieces from the boy's lunch. He kept on breaking them. Everyone had enough to eat. Do you know anyone else who can do that? Only Jesus can do it! He is God's Son!

WHAT DO YOU SEE?
How many rolls of bread do you see? How many fish do you see? Where are the people Jesus will feed with the lunch?

A TIME TO SHARE
1. *Why did the boy bring this food?*
2. *What did Jesus do with it?*
3. *How can Jesus do this? Who is He?*
4. *Are you glad Jesus is God's Son?*

139

Let's Go on a Hayride
My Favorite Thing: Hay for a Hayride

Who doesn't love to go on a hayride? Hayrides are for cool autumn days. Don't you wish you were here too? This boy and the girls are having a wonderful time. They love to smell the fresh hay. They love to feel the hay and toss some up and watch it fall again. And don't you like to hear the horse go *clop clop* when you're on a hayride. This is one of my favorite things. Is it yours?

WHAT DO YOU SEE?
Do you think this is in a city? Why do you think it is in the country? Where is the hay? Where is the horse? Who do you think is driving?

A TIME TO SHARE
1. *Why is a hayride fun?*
2. *What do you see on a hayride? What do you smell? What do you hear?*
3. *Who do you like with you then?*

Look at That Pumpkin!

My Favorite Thing: That Pumpkin

It can't be just any old pumpkin, can it? Not when you are choosing a special one for Halloween. Father and Mother will help choose just the right one. It can't be too big or too small. It can't be too wide or too high. It must be just right. The boy has found the right one for him. The girl has found the right one for her. And Father has found the right one for the family. But who do you think will pay for all these pumpkins?

A TIME TO SHARE

1. *What is this family buying?*
2. *What do you think they will do with their pumpkins?*
3. *Do you like to buy pumpkins too?*

WHAT DO YOU SEE?
How many pumpkins can you count? Which one did the boy choose? Which one did the girl choose? Which one did Father choose? Which pumpkin has a face carved on it?

Autumn Leaves

My Favorite Thing: Leaves to Rake

You can see that this family is having fun. Don't you like to rake leaves into a big pile? Don't you like to jump into that big pile of leaves? Do you suppose Mother is making hot chocolate or cookies or something special to eat on an autumn day? This family is having fun together. And that's really the way to have fun, isn't it?

A TIME TO SHARE

1. *What is this family doing?*
2. *Why is it more fun to do this together?*
3. *Are you glad when you can do things together with your family? What do you do?*

WHAT DO YOU SEE?

How do you know this is autumn? Why isn't it spring or summer? Why isn't it winter? Where did these leaves come from?

Thank You, God, for Turkey

My Favorite Thing: Thanksgiving Turkey

There it is! Mother and Father have worked for hours to get that turkey ready for Thanksgiving dinner. Have you ever watched Mother make dressing? You know how much time she spends doing it. But how long does it take you to eat it? Now look at Father. What do you think he is getting ready to do? What do you think the boy and girl are ready to do?

A TIME TO SHARE

1. *What do you like best about Thanksgiving dinner? Why?*
2. *What should you do before you eat?*
3. *Why should you thank God for food?*

WHAT DO YOU SEE?
Point to some things that tell you this is Thanksgiving time. Point to something else this family will eat for dinner. What kind of pies do you think those are?

143

Father Is Home!

My Favorite Thing: A Hug

Father is home! Father is home! You can see that he has been away for a few days. Guess who gets the first hug? Mother is already there, and Father has a special hug for her. Then the girl is next. She will get a special hug too. What is Father trying to say when he hugs Mother? What is he trying to say when he hugs his girl? Do you suppose he also says out loud, "I love you"?

WHAT DO YOU SEE?
What is that next to Father? Does he take this to his work? Or does he take this suitcase when he goes on a trip? Where do you think Father has been?

A TIME TO SHARE
1. *Are you glad for a special hug from someone you love? Why?*
2. *What does a hug tell you?*
3. *Have you hugged Father or Mother today?*

144

Don't Throw That Ball!

My Favorite Thing: Our Blocks

This boy and girl are having fun together. Wouldn't you like to play with them? They would let you put some blocks on the tower. Do you think you could put the last one on before the tower falls? You'd better hurry. That naughty boy with the ball is about to knock over the tower. Do you think that will be fun for them? What do you think they will say to that naughty boy?

A TIME TO SHARE

1. *What are the boy and girl making?*
2. *What is the other boy doing?*
3. *What would you like to say to him?*
4. *Why should he not throw the ball?*

WHAT DO YOU SEE?
How many blocks can you count? How many words can you make with the letters you see?

That Sheep!

My Favorite Thing: The Lost Sheep

This foolish sheep wandered away from the others. Now it doesn't know where to go. It doesn't know how to get back to the shepherd. It doesn't know how to get back to the other sheep. But don't worry. The shepherd knows it is lost. He is coming to find it. When he does, he will take it home where it will be safe. Are you glad he will do that?

WHAT DO YOU SEE?
How many sheep do you see? Where are all the others? Why do you think this is not the shepherd's home?

A TIME TO SHARE
1. *Why is this sheep here?*
2. *Where should it be?*
3. *Who will come to find it?*
4. *What will the shepherd do with it?*

146

Hurry!

My Favorite Thing: My Comb

Hurry! You'll be late for school if you don't. That's what Mother is telling this boy. Don't you think he should hurry then? What will happen if he doesn't? The boy is trying to hurry. But he has one more thing to do. He must comb his hair. What would his friends say if he does not do that? What would Mother say? The boy is glad that he has a comb. It helps him look nice for his friends and family. That makes his comb a special friend, doesn't it?

WHAT DO YOU SEE?
What time is it? Why do you think this is morning and not night? What is Mother holding in her hands? What will the boy do with them?

A TIME TO SHARE
1. *What is the boy doing?*
2. *Why is he glad for his comb?*
3. *What do you use to help you look better for friends and family?*

Listen to that Horn

My Favorite Thing: A Horn to Blow

There is something exciting about a horn. If you have a horn, you know how much fun it is to blow it. Look at this boy. He is making more noise than he can make with anything else. Could that be why he is having so much fun? But look at Father. He isn't having much fun, is he? And what about the boy's brother? Is he having fun? Puppy doesn't seem to be having much fun either. Look at him howl. When you have fun with horns and noise, it's a good idea to think of others around you. You want them to have fun too, don't you?

WHAT DO YOU SEE?
How many faces do you see? Which one is a happy face? Which ones are not so happy?

A TIME TO SHARE
1. *Why is that one boy having fun?*
2. *Why are the others not so happy?*
3. *What should you remember when you want to make a lot of noise?*

Home from School

My Favorite Thing: Cookies and Milk

Do you see what Mother has for her girl? You probably like to eat cookies when you come home from school too. What is your favorite kind? Can you tell how they taste? Of course a glass of milk tastes so good with cookies. Why do you think this girl has just come home from school? She hasn't hung up her coat yet, has she? What else do you see on the floor? And what is she still holding in her hand? Do you think she will hang up her coat and put away her mittens soon? You would do that, wouldn't you?

A TIME TO SHARE

1. *What do you do first when you come home from school?*
2. *When Mother gives you something special, what do you say to her?*

WHAT DO YOU SEE?

What room of the house is this? How do you know? Can you point to some things that you would not find in the living room?

Look at My New Shoes

My Favorite Thing: New Shoes

This is always a fun time, isn't it? Mother knows it is time to buy some new shoes for her boy and girl. You can always tell by looking at the old shoes, can't you? The girl likes the new shoes she has put on. They look so new and clean. They feel good on her feet. The boy is glad his sister has found the right shoes. Now he can try some on. Do you think he will find the right ones? Do you think he will be glad when he does?

A TIME TO SHARE

1. *What is the girl doing?*
2. *Why do you think she looks happy?*
3. *What do you think she is saying?*
4. *What do you say when you get new shoes?*

WHAT DO YOU SEE?

What kind of store do you think this is? How do you know? Why do you think it is not a grocery store? Why do you think this is not the living room at home?

Jesus Knows Everything

My Favorite Thing: Nets Filled with Fish

Look at all those fish! Can you count them? Someone has caught them in a big net. Do you know who did that? Jesus could tell you. He saw some of His friends fishing. They fished all night. But they did not catch one fish. Then Jesus told them to put their nets down in one place. When they did, look what happened! Now you know that Jesus can do things that no one else can do. That's because He is God's Son.

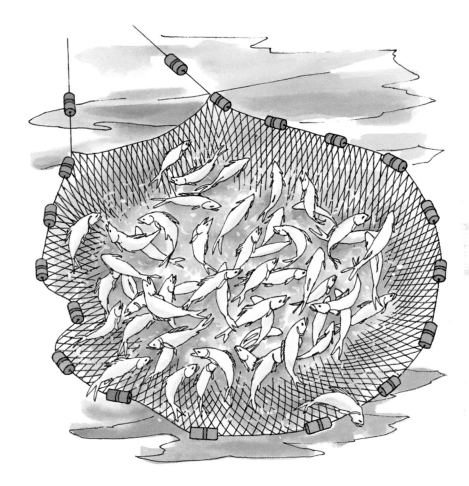

A TIME TO SHARE

1. How did these fish get into the net?

2. Who knew where to find the fish?

3. How did Jesus know?

4. What does Jesus know about you? Why?

WHAT DO YOU SEE?

Do you see the floats around the edge of the net? They kept one edge of the net on top of the water. The other edge sank down. Then fish got caught in the net.

Welcome Back!

My Favorite Thing: Airplane

"Father is back! Father is back!" That's what this boy is saying. He is glad that Father is on that airplane. Now Father will stay home with him and Mother for awhile. Of course, Mother is glad too! She is always glad when she and Father and the boy can be home. Then they can do special things together. Are you glad when you and your family can do things together?

WHAT DO YOU SEE?
Is this on a farm? Is it downtown? Why not? Where are these people? How do you know? Is the airplane flying? What is it doing?

A TIME TO SHARE
1. *Who is on that airplane?*
2. *Why are Mother and the boy happy to have Father come home?*
3. *Will Father be glad to be home?*

152

A Toasty, Cozy Night

My Favorite Thing: Fire in the Fireplace

Grandfather is telling the best story ever. Don't you think he is having fun? Of course, the boy is having fun too. He loves to listen to Grandfather's stories. But these stories sound better when there's a fire in the fireplace. It's a cold winter night outside and the boy is happy to stay with Grandfather and Grandmother. They are happy to have him with them. Grandmother is in the kitchen. Do you think she is making hot chocolate or popcorn? Of course, these people will sit up late. They will talk about many wonderful things as they sit by the fire in the fireplace.

A TIME TO SHARE

1. *What is Grandfather doing?*
2. *What is the boy doing?*
3. *Why do you think each is happy?*
4. *Why do you like a fire like this?*

WHAT DO YOU SEE?

Point to the fire in the fireplace. What else do you see that tells you this is winter? Why do you think this is night?

What Are You Knitting?

My Favorite Thing: Mother's Yarn

Kitty is having so much fun with Mother's yarn. That's because Mother doesn't see what Kitty is doing. What do you think she will do when she sees Kitty? But look at the other end of Mother's yarn. What is Mother doing? Don't you think the girl is having fun? Don't you think she would like to know how to do this? She will! Mother is teaching her how. Before long the girl will be making beautiful things too. Would you like to do this?

WHAT DO YOU SEE?
How many balls of yarn do you see? What else do you see that will help Mother knit with the yarn?

A TIME TO SHARE
1. *What is Mother doing?*
2. *How is she helping the girl?*
3. *Why do you think the girl is glad to be here with Mother? Would you be glad?*

What's That Noise?
My Favorite Thing: My Flashlight

What's that noise? Do you hear it? The boy hears it. You know he is frightened. Who wouldn't be when he knows something, or someone, is in his bedroom. It's dark. It's too dark to see what's there. That's why this boy is frightened. But look! The boy has found his flashlight. Now he will not be frightened anymore. Do you know why?

WHAT DO YOU SEE?
What do you see in the boy's room? Why couldn't the boy see without his flashlight? How do you know this is night? Point to some things that tell you.

A TIME TO SHARE
1. *What is the boy holding?*
2. *How does it give light?*
3. *What else do you see that gives light? Which one did God make?*

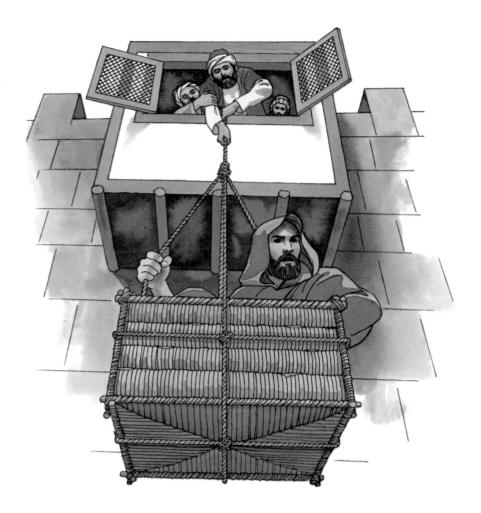

Friends Who Help

My Favorite Thing: Saul's Basket

Look at that man in the basket. His name is Saul. Some men want to kill him. They are angry because he became Jesus' friend. They did not want him to do that. But Saul has some friends who want to help him. They are helping him get out of this city. Do you see how they are doing this? They put Saul into a big basket. Now they are letting the basket down. They are putting Saul down from the big wall of the city. Now he can go away. Those bad men can't hurt him now.

WHAT DO YOU SEE?
Point to the basket. Who is in it? How are the friends letting the basket down? Do you see the wall of the city? Do you see the window?

A TIME TO SHARE
1. *Why is this man in a basket?*
2. *Who is helping him get away?*
3. *Why do some men want to hurt him?*
4. *Are you glad for friends who help?*

156

Together

My Favorite Thing: Candlelight

Now this looks like fun. Would you like to be here? Would you like to have Mother put her arm around you and talk about the candlelight? Candlelight is warm and soft, isn't it? Think how it would feel if the room were completely dark. Would you be glad for the warm, soft light of the candle then? Of course you would. And you would be especially glad that Mother was with you.

A TIME TO SHARE

1. Who is with this girl?

2. Why is the girl glad that Mother is with her?

3. Do you like to be with Mother? Why?

WHAT DO YOU SEE?

Do you see a light bulb? Do you see a flashlight? What do you see that gives light? How would you tell someone about this light?

It's Snowing

My Favorite Thing: The First Snowflakes

It's snowing! It's snowing! Who doesn't get excited when the first snowflakes come each winter? Do you? This boy and girl do. You can see how excited they are. They are running to catch the snowflakes. Do you think they will?

A TIME TO SHARE

1. *Who makes the snowflakes?*
2. *Are they all the same?*
3. *What would you like to tell God about His beautiful snowflakes?*

WHAT DO YOU SEE?
Why do you think this is winter? What are the boy and girl wearing? Do you wear these things in summer? Why isn't Mother wearing a coat?

Do You See My Picture?

My Favorite Thing: Crayons

Do you like to color with crayons? Look! There is a red one, and yellow, and green. What other colors can you find? This boy and girl are having fun, aren't they? One of them is coloring neatly. Can you show which one? What would you like to say to the girl about being neat? What would you like to say to the boy?

A TIME TO SHARE

1. What are the girl and boy doing?

2. Are they having fun?

3. Why do you have fun with crayons?

4. What do you do with them?

WHAT DO YOU SEE?
Is it summer or winter? How do you know? Is it morning or afternoon? How do you know?

Let Me Help You
My Favorite Thing: A Snow Shovel

Now here is something you don't do in the summer. But when winter comes, it's time to get out the snow shovel. Father is shoveling the snow from the sidewalk. Someone has to do it. So he is glad when his boy comes out to help. The boy has a snow shovel too. It is not as big as Father's. He will not shovel as much snow as Father. But Father doesn't care. He is glad to have the boy with him. He is glad the boy wants to be a helper. You like to be a helper too, don't you?

WHAT DO YOU SEE?
What is that big thing coming down the street? Why can't it shovel the sidewalk for Father? Why can't the boy use that to help Father?

A TIME TO SHARE
1. *What are Father and the boy doing?*
2. *Why do they seem happy?*
3. *Why do you like to help Father or Mother? What do you do to help?*

Sailing Far Away

My Favorite Thing: Paul's Ship

Would you think it fun to sail on this ship? It could be. But it wasn't fun for Paul. He was going far away from home. He was going to see Caesar. This man was like a king. He would decide if Paul should go to prison. He would decide if Paul should die. Now you know why this trip was not fun for Paul. Now you know why it wasn't fun to sail on this ship.

A TIME TO SHARE

1. Where is Paul going?

2. What will Caesar do?

3. Why is this trip not fun for Paul?

4. What would you like to tell Paul?

WHAT DO YOU SEE?

Where are the sails on the ship? Why did the ship have sails? How many men do you see on the ship? Which way is the ship going?

There's a Bird in My Clock
My Favorite Thing: A Cuckoo Clock

Do you see that funny little bird? It is called a cuckoo. This girl likes to watch it hop out its little door. It says *cuckoo, cuckoo.* Every time the big hand points to twelve the little bird comes out. Do you know why? Father is telling his girl why. What do you think he is saying?

WHAT DO YOU SEE?

What number is the big hand pointing to? What number is the little hand pointing to? What time is it? How many times will the bird say *cuckoo?*

A TIME TO SHARE

1. *What is Father telling the girl?*
2. *What would you like to ask him?*
3. *How many times would the bird say cuckoo at noon?*

162

A Frosty Morning

My Favorite Thing: Frost on My Window

You can see that it's a cold winter day. Look through that window. Do you see those boys and girls playing? They wouldn't do those things on a summer day, would they? And they would not dress that way on a summer day. Look at this boy and girl indoors. They have found something else that you see only on a cold winter day. Do you see it? This boy and girl like to look at the frost on the window. They like to trace the patterns in the frost. God makes some wonderful things, doesn't He?

WHAT DO YOU SEE?
What do you see that you would not see in the summer? Why wouldn't you see these things in the summer?

A TIME TO SHARE
1. *Can you make frost? Who makes it?*
2. *Why do you like to look at frost on your window? What do you see?*
3. *Why can God make things you can't?*

Zipping My Zipper

My Favorite Thing: Zippers that Zip

Aren't you glad for a zipper that zips? Sometimes zippers don't zip. Then we pull or tug or push. Sometimes that makes us angry, doesn't it? So we really are glad for a zipper that zips. How would you put on your coat if it didn't? How could you go outside to play? That boy outside has a zipper that zips. He wouldn't be out there if it didn't. The boy inside hopes his zipper zips. Then he can go out and make a snowman with his brother. Aren't you glad for a zipper that zips?

A TIME TO SHARE

1. *What does a zipper do?*
2. *If all of these zippers did not zip, what could these people not do?*
3. *Thank Mother for helping you!*

WHAT DO YOU SEE?

How many zippers do you see in this picture? Can you name each thing that has a zipper?

164

Friends Outside My Window

My Favorite Thing: Our Bird Feeder

Do you see those little birds? They get hungry, just as you do. But when winter comes it is not so easy to find food. This mother and her boy know that. So they help the birds by giving them something to eat. It doesn't look much like your dinner table. But the birds like it that way. They really would not want to eat at your dinner table. Of course, you wouldn't want to eat what they are eating either. That's the way God made birds and you. Isn't He a wonderful God?

A TIME TO SHARE

1. What are the birds doing?

2. Who gave them this food?

3. How do you get your food?

4. Who gives us all our food? How?

WHAT DO YOU SEE?
How many birds do you see at the bird feeder? What shows you that this is winter? How do you know this is outside? How do you know these people are inside?

At Grandmother's House

My Favorite Thing: Grandmother's Toy Chest

Do you like to go to Grandmother's house? This boy does. Grandmother gives him a big hug. So does Grandfather. Then the boy runs to a special place at Grandmother's house. Do you know where it is? Look! The boy is already there. He didn't even take time to hang up his scarf and gloves. Of course he will do that later, won't he? But now he will play with the toys in Grandmother's toy chest. Do you ever do this?

WHAT DO YOU SEE?
Who are the five people in this picture? Point to each one. What toys do you see? What else do you see?

A TIME TO SHARE
1. *Why is Grandmother so happy?*
2. *Why is the boy so happy?*
3. *Mother thinks the boy should hang up his clothes first. Do you?*

A Place to Sleep

My Favorite Thing: Baby Jesus' Manger

This doesn't look much like a bed, does it? But it was. This is where Baby Jesus slept after He was born. It wasn't made to be a bed. Some men made it to be a manger. That's where cows ate. But there was no other place for Baby Jesus to sleep. Mary and Joseph could not find a room that night. They had to stay in a stable. Now you know why Baby Jesus was born there. Now you know why He slept in this manger.

A TIME TO SHARE

1. *What is this?*
2. *Who slept here?*
3. *Why didn't He sleep in a bed?*
4. *What would you tell Baby Jesus?*

WHAT DO YOU SEE?
Can you find the straw? Do you see the long cloth? Mary wrapped the cloth around Baby Jesus. Then she put Him here to sleep.

Up We Go!

My Favorite Thing: An Escalator

Now here is something we all like to do. It's fun to go shopping with Mother and Father. But it's especially fun when we can ride up the escalator. It's fun to ride down the escalator too. Who wants to walk up or down all those steps when we can ride? This boy and girl like to look down into the store while they ride. Everything seems to change as they go higher and higher. You've seen that happen, haven't you? Of course, the most fun of all is to get to the floor where you want to go. Is that where they sell toys? Or is it where they sell clothing? What do you think?

WHAT DO YOU SEE?
How do you know this family is riding up? How would they look if they were riding down? What does the store sell on the floor they are leaving?

A TIME TO SHARE
1. *What is this family doing?*
2. *Why is this fun for them?*
3. *What would you say if you were here?*

168

Grandmother's Gift

My Favorite Thing: My New Quilt

This girl is getting a special gift. Do you see what Grandmother has made for her? Grandmother is happy that she could make this beautiful quilt for the girl. That tells the girl that she loves her and wants to do something good for her. Mother is happy too. She is glad that Grandmother loves her girl. Of course the girl is very happy. Who wouldn't want a beautiful quilt that Grandmother made?

WHAT DO YOU SEE?
What kind of machine is that? How did Grandmother use that? Can you find the thread? What else do you see?

A TIME TO SHARE
1. *Why is this girl so happy?*
2. *What did Grandmother do for her?*
3. *What do you think the girl is saying?*
4. *What would you say?*

Something Hot This Morning
My Favorite Thing: Hot Chocolate

It's cold outside. You can see the snow piled up everywhere. But we all like a beautiful winter morning, don't we? It's fun to go outside. This family thinks so. They have been outside making a snowman. Of course, they could have been sledding. Or they could have gone skating. Now their faces are tingling from the cold air. So it's time to come inside and get warm. Mmmmm. Do you see what they are drinking? You like to drink hot chocolate on a winter morning too, don't you?

WHAT DO YOU SEE?
How many cups of hot chocolate do you see? Point to the things Mother used to make this hot chocolate. Can you find the marshmallows? What are they for?

A TIME TO SHARE
1. *What is this family doing?*
2. *Why does this taste so good now?*
3. *Why would it not taste as good in the summer?*

170

Cookie Fun

My Favorite Thing: Cookie Dough

Would you like to reach out and touch that cookie dough? Would you like to nibble on it? This girl will probably do both of those things. But she will also help Mother cut some cookies from the dough. Do you see the cookie cutter in her hand? What will the shape of those cookies be? How do you know? This girl and her mother like to work together. It is fun to do special things with Mother, isn't it?

A TIME TO SHARE

1. *What is Mother holding? What will that do to the cookie dough?*
2. *What do you like to do with cookie dough? What do you do with cookies?*

WHAT DO YOU SEE?

Point to some things that Mother used to make the cookie dough. Can you name each one? The big jar holds something sweet. What do you think that is?

Look What I Brought

My Favorite Thing: A Christmas Gift

It's that time of year again. What would Christmas be without Christmas gifts? This girl is surprised when she opens her front door. There is a special friend smiling at her. You can see what this friend has in her hands. It's a special gift, wrapped in pretty paper. This girl is so happy. It doesn't matter what's in the package. She is happy that her friend loves her. She is happy that her friend wants to give her something. Gifts don't have to be big. They don't have to cost a lot of money. But they must say, "I love you."

A TIME TO SHARE

1. *What does the girl have in her hands?*
2. *Why has she brought this gift?*
3. *What is more important than the gift?*
4. *Why do you like to give gifts?*

WHAT DO YOU SEE?
Point to some things that tell you that this is not summer. What wouldn't you see then?

That Bright Star

My Favorite Thing: The Star the Wise Men Saw

Look at that bright star in the sky! It was the brightest star in all the sky. It must have been brighter than any star has ever been. These wise men had never seen a star like that before. That's why they followed it. They knew it was a special star. They knew it would show them the way to find Jesus. Would you follow a star like that?

A TIME TO SHARE

1. What are these men doing?

2. Where are they going?

3. Would you like to go with them? Why?

4. Would you like to have seen Baby Jesus?

WHAT DO YOU SEE?
How many men do you see? What are they riding? What are they following? Point to the star.

Warm, Fuzzy Mittens
My Favorite Thing: My Mittens

If that girl takes off her new mittens her hands will get cold, won't they? But she won't take them off now until she gets home. The girl likes her new mittens. Mother has just bought them for her. Look how she is putting her fuzzy, warm mittens up to her face. Now her mittens are helping to keep her face warm too. And they feel so soft and furry. Do you think Mother is happy? She is glad to see her girl like her warm new mittens. Are you glad for your mittens too?

WHAT DO YOU SEE?
Why do you think this is a cold winter day? Point to some things that tell you that. How would these things be different in the summer?

A TIME TO SHARE
1. *How do you know that the girl likes her mittens? Why does she?*
2. *How do you know that Mother is happy? Why is she?*

Listen! Do You Hear It?

My Favorite Thing: Grandfather's Watch

Isn't it wonderful to go to Grandfather's house? Grandfather has many things that the boy does not have at his house. Do you see some of them? The boy is holding one in his hands. What do you think he hears? What do you think he sees? Does Grandfather's watch feel hard and shiny or soft and cuddly? The boy likes to listen to Grandfather's watch. He likes to look at it. When he does this, he thinks of Grandfather. That helps him remember how much he loves Grandfather.

A TIME TO SHARE

1. *What is the boy doing?*
2. *Why do you think Grandfather is glad to have the boy with him?*
3. *How do you know the boy loves him?*

WHAT DO YOU SEE?

What do you see at Grandfather's house? Can you tell what each thing is? Can you tell how Grandfather uses each thing you see? What does his watch tell him?

175

Listen to the Bells

My Favorite Thing: Bells

Listen! Do you hear what I hear? What is it? Do you hear some bells? This mother and girl hear them. They like to listen to the bells. Do you suppose that girl's brother or sister is ringing one of those bells? You can see that the boys and girls are having fun ringing the bells. But they are doing something else too. When they ring the bells, they play music. This music tells about Jesus. Would you like to listen? Would you like to ring bells that tell about Jesus?

WHAT DO YOU SEE?
Where are these people? How do you know? How many bells can you find? Point to each one and tell whether a boy or girl is ringing it.

A TIME TO SHARE
1. *What are the boys and girls doing?*
2. *How do these bells make music?*
3. *How do they tell about Jesus?*
4. *Why do you like to hear bells?*

Look What I'm Doing

My Favorite Thing: My Christmas Stocking

Look at this girl. Do you know what she is doing? Mother does. She would be glad to help the girl hang up her stocking. But the girl wants to do it herself. You can see how the girl must stand up on her toes to hang it. But she doesn't mind. She knows that her stocking will help her think about Christmas. Perhaps someone will put a special gift in her stocking too. Who do you think would do that?

WHAT DO YOU SEE?

What special time is coming? How do you know? Point to some things that you would see at Christmas. Why wouldn't you see these things at Easter?

A TIME TO SHARE

1. *What is the girl doing?*
2. *Why doesn't Mother help her?*
3. *What may the girl find in her stocking?*
4. *Why do we give each other gifts?*

177

Gifts for Jesus

My Favorite Thing: The Wise Men's Gifts

Do you like to get gifts for your birthday? Do you like to get them at Christmas? What do you do first? Do you tear off the paper? That's fun, isn't it? But you don't see paper on these gifts, do you? People did not wrap gifts that way in Jesus' time. But they did give special gifts. The wise men brought these gifts to Jesus. One gift is gold. Another is a spice called myrrh. The other is a spice called frankincense. These gifts cost a lot of money. But the wise men did not care. They wanted to give the best gifts to Jesus. Isn't that a good idea?

A TIME TO SHARE

1. *Who brought the special gifts?*
2. *Who were they for?*
3. *Why were these gifts special?*
4. *What would you like to give Jesus?*

WHAT DO YOU SEE?
What do you think is in those two jars? Where is the gold? How many pieces of gold can you find? Who is Mary holding?

178

Sledding Fun

My Favorite Thing: My Sled

What is more exciting than sledding down a hill on a winter day? You can feel the wind on your face. And the snow flies up from the runners of the sled. This boy's cheeks are rosy red from the cold and snow. But he doesn't mind. Not when he can go sledding with his friends. When sledding time is over, he will go into the house. Perhaps Mother will have some hot chocolate and cookies. Would you like to go sledding with him? Would you like to share his hot chocolate and cookies?

A TIME TO SHARE

1. *Which boys and girls are having fun?*
2. *Which one is not sharing his sled with his little brother?*
3. *Why should he share?*

WHAT DO YOU SEE?
How many boys and girls are sledding today? What time of year is this? Is it summer? Is it winter? How do you know? What do you like to do in the winter?

Snowflake Fun

My Favorite Thing: Snowflakes

There are so many things you can do with snowflakes. When they pile up high, you can slide on your sled or make a big snowman. You can even run and catch the snowflakes as they come falling down. That's what some of these boys and girls are doing. And look at that boy on his knees. Is he eating some of this fresh new snow? Father isn't playing with the snow. He is doing something else. Do you know what he is doing? Snow is fun, don't you think?

WHAT DO YOU SEE?
Point to some of the snowflakes. Do you see the snowman? Can you find some snowdrifts or piles?

A TIME TO SHARE
1. *What is Father doing?*
2. *What are the boys and girls doing?*
3. *What do you like to do in the snow?*
4. *Is this winter or summer? Why?*

Mr. Snowman

My Favorite Thing: Snowman

Mr. Snowman came here today. Do you see him? Father rolled up three big balls of snow. Then he and the boy put a hat on Mr. Snowman and a scarf around his neck. Do you think they did that to keep him warm? Now look what the boy is putting on Mr. Snowman for a nose. Father and the boy are having so much fun together. But that other boy and girl are not having fun together, are they? Do you know why not?

A TIME TO SHARE

1. What are Father and the boy doing?

2. Why do you think they are having fun?

3. What do you like to do with your father or mother?

WHAT DO YOU SEE?
What time of the year is this? How do you know? Point to 10 things that you would not see out here in the yard if this were summer.

Happy Valentine's Day!
My Favorite Thing: Valentines

What are all those hearts on the table? This boy and girl like to make valentines. They like to send some to their special friends. They like to give one to each special person in their family. Who do you think those special family members are? Can you name some? You can see that the boy and girl will mail some of the valentines. Some friends or family must live far away. Do you like to send valentines?

WHAT DO YOU SEE?
How do you know that the boy and girl will mail some of their valentines? How do you know that they are making their valentines instead of buying them?

A TIME TO SHARE
1. *How many valentines do you see?*
2. *What else do you see? Can you name each thing they used?*
3. *What does a valentine tell someone?*

WHAT YOU SHOULD KNOW ABOUT THIS BOOK

MY FAVORITE THINGS TO SEE AND SHARE is a book about those wonderful things that should be an important part of every child's life. You treasure many as part of your childhood and want them for your child too. This is a book about the fabric of childhood and those beautiful threads, my favorite things, which contribute so significantly to the total design.

Childhood

Childhood is not merely preparation for adult life, although that is one important function. We must recognize the value of childhood for the sake of childhood as well as its important preparation for adult living.

God had a wonderful idea when He planned for us to go through childhood. It was His idea, you know. He could have planned it in such a way that we would enter the world as mature adults and live out the full term as adults. But He didn't. God thought it good that we become children first.

Childhood as Preparation for Adult Living

We all recognize the value of growing into adult living. We grow slowly, accepting more and more responsibility and we become increasingly capable of handling larger tasks. This slow growth and slow positioning toward responsibility keeps us from facing enormous demands overnight.

God planned growth through age levels of childhood from infancy to adulthood. Step by step we move through each important stage of growth. At

183

each stage we expect to accomplish certain things which are characteristic of that age level.

Caring parents go beyond the basic demands of an age level and provide a rich assortment of experiences which help their child mature more rapidly than his peers. But the wise parent keeps these experiences somewhat within the child's level of growth, giving a child more and better experiences for his own level of growth, but not trying to force the child to perform far beyond his age level.

Growth regarded as normal for each level is best experienced at that level. Except for a gifted child, we expect two-year-olds to grow as twos, not as ten-year-olds. And we expect ten-year-olds to grow as tens, not as twos.

Maturity in adult life comes from fulfilling important maturing experiences at each age level. We must never accept the idea that childhood is less important than adulthood merely because a child appears to be a "little kid." In the total tapestry of life, what is accomplished at the age of two is as important as what is accomplished at the age of twenty-two, or thirty-two, or sixty-two.

Childhood for the Sake of Childhood

Preparation for adult living is an important part of childhood. But childhood for the sake of childhood is equally important. Or to put it another way, childhood is important not only for what we can get out of it, but also for what we can put into it.

If we always look on childhood as only a way leading somewhere (toward adulthood), we will miss those marvelous delights of childhood itself. Let's help our children enjoy being children, and let's find our delight in seeing them do that. Being a child is as important as becoming an adult. When we accept that, we accept a child as a total person, not as an incomplete one.

The Erosion of Childhood

Society is too often not in tune with this idea. Childhood becomes a means to an end—growing up and getting into adult productivity. Thus, the faster we get to adulthood, the better it is.

That's why society is making our children grow up too fast. It is trying to force children to jump over certain important stages and experiences that are vital to an age level. Peer pressure sometimes moves in and tempts our children to want to rush up the age ladder too quickly. Even thoughtless parents, proud of their "achieving" children, encourage them to move beyond the level of their normal growth. Wouldn't it be better to provide more and richer experiences within a level of growth rather than pushing a child too far beyond his or her normal growth level?

Of course, we must recognize that there are truly gifted children. Gifted children deserve opportunities to grow within their capacity to grow.

The erosion of childhood is a serious problem today. It is so serious that secular educators and communicators have published a number of books and articles expressing concern. They are concerned that teen lifestyle and problems are moving downward into the childhood years, and that children are being encouraged to move quickly upward beyond their norm.

For example, many teens are burned out on sex before they reach the maturity level to marry. So where then is the delight of new love in marriage? Problems with alcohol, drugs, and explicit language have moved downward. What were high school problems when we parents were in school are too often junior high or elementary school problems today.

Athletic competition has in too many cases ceased to be fun, teamwork, and exercise builders, but has copied professional athletics. Greater emphasis on winning at any cost rather than sportsmanship and teamwork forces children in these programs to think like adults.

Girls often opt for adult underclothing before they are physically or psychologically ready for it. Television projects a strong current of adult themes, adult language, and adult sexual information and ever younger children hear and see this daily. Video recorders, which can be a marvelous aid to education and entertainment, can also host a smorgasbord of X-rated materials and put them within the reach of our children.

Also, through TV, children are exposed daily to adult problems in explicit detail. Violence, murder, rape, sexuality, divorce, and even incest are laid be-

fore the audience, which too often includes children.

Children too often can't wait for the prerogatives of the next age level. These include 6-year-olds wanting to be 10 so they can stay up later or dress in a different way or enjoy some other privilege. Also, 14-year-olds can't wait until they are 16 to get their driver's license and the privilege of using the family car.

Psychologists and psychiatrists warn that the pressures of what some call the "hurried child syndrome" may produce unusual stress, with fear of failure and fear of not measuring up.

This book is designed to fill an important gap. It not only acknowledges the need to let children be children, but takes children and parents together through 174 delightful experiences that should be part of childhood. These experiences are part of growing up, but they are also part of the delight of being a child while the childhood years are here.

Sensory Rich Experiences

The favorite things of childhood in this book are sensory rich. They are things a child loves to smell, touch, taste, hear, or see. What child should not experience the smell of pancakes when he wakes up, or hear the sounds of a rooster crowing? What child should not experience the soft feel of a baby chick against the cheek? What child should not feel the tingle of snow blowing up from the runners of his sled as he races down a snowy hill? What child should not taste hot buttered popcorn or a peppermint and chocolate ice cream cone?

You will remember many of these favorite things from your own childhood because they were sensory rich to you. Think back on the most important memories of your life. You will likely find many of them in this book.

Together

The favorite things in this book are things parent and child or teacher and child should experience together. Or some should be experienced with friends. An ice cream cone or bag of hot buttered popcorn is a delight. But it is a richer experience when Father or Mother or family is together somewhere to buy it.

You will find a strong thread of family together-

ness in this book. The child sees himself in a loving relationship with fathers, mothers, grandfathers, grandmothers, friends, teachers, or others who are a warm and wonderful part of the child's life.

Read-to-Me

Another part of the togetherness emphasis is the read-to-me nature of this book. This book will do its work best when parent or teacher reads to the child. The read-to-me experience is one of togetherness, of feeling the warmth of presence, hearing a loving voice, talking with someone the child loves, and knowing that person is there to share this delightful experience with him. Read-to-me is a two-way street, with parent or teacher reaching out to share while the child reaches out to listen and learn.

Because of the strong read-to-me emphasis, this book uses oral vocabulary rather than the child's "learning to read" vocabulary. It also uses imagery and sentences more often associated with oral communication rather than those associated with beginning reading.

Tense Change

Occasionally you will encounter a deliberate change of tense within a "story," especially in the Bible material. This recognizes a past action along with the child's involvement in a current happening. It helps to involve your child now in an event pictured in the past, or a past action which led to the pictured scene.

Picture Reading

This book has 144 colorful pictures of everyday situations, each picturing one of "my favorite things." In addition, it has 30 Bible-time pictures, each picturing one of "my favorite things" mentioned in a Bible story.

The primary emphasis of the storytelling portion is picture reading. Instead of reading a story, you read a picture. Out of that, you and your child discover a story. The story unfolds as you look at the picture and "read" it together.

As you read each picture together, you will begin to focus on one of "my favorite things," which we are sure will be one of your favorite things too.

Through this picture reading experience, you and your child will desire favorite things and will seek ways to enjoy these together. Picture reading is a blend of the visual and verbal, helping you and your child to enter into true-to-life experiences vicariously as you sit together in your living room or Sunday School room.

Discovery Power

With each picture is a question and answer feature called WHAT DO YOU SEE? It focuses on the little things in the picture which you may easily pass by

too quickly. By finding and focusing on these little things, you and your child develop "discovery power" which may be used in everyday life. It will help you discover those little things we pass by too quickly every day. And it will help you find meaning in each one.

Discovery power helps your child become more observant. He or she will look for clues that will tell why the scene is one season instead of another, or why it is one room rather than another, or why it is one time of the day instead of another.

Discovery power also encourages and stimulates

imagination, observation, and creativity. These are the marks of a man or woman of sensitivity instead of insensitivity. We know you want this for your child.

A Time to Share

Also with each picture is another question and answer feature called A TIME TO SHARE. Through three or four questions the child is encouraged to talk about the situation he has just "read." You will talk together about the favorite thing you have seen, what this means to each of you, and how you will respond to it.

Dialogue with parent or teacher begins and the child develops the art of thinking through something he or she has just experienced.

This feature helps a child develop perspective, asking how or why and what that means to him. It helps him think about God and how He relates to that favorite thing and to the child himself.

Prayer Partnership

Like previous books in this series, this book is a prayer partnership. We have prayed for your child and for you as you use this book. We have prayed for the ministry of this book as we have written and developed it. Now you will have the opportunity to join us in prayer, to pray for yourself as you use the book, and for your child as you share the book. And of course, you will want to encourage your child to pray about those important new things that he or she learns.

DATE DUE

BW. 1601